Resolving conflict IN MARRIAGE

D1413417

Resolving conflict IN MARRIAGE

Darrell L. Hines

WHITAKER HOUSE

RESOLVING CONFLICT IN MARRIAGE

Christian Faith Fellowship Ministries
8605 West Good Hope Road
Milwaukee, WI 53224

ISBN: 0-88368-729-1
Printed in the United States of America
© 2001 by Darrell L. Hines

Whitaker House
30 Hunt Valley Circle
New Kensington, PA 15068
Visit our web site at: www.whitakerhouse.com

Library of Congress Cataloging-in-Publication Data

Hines, Darrell, 1958–
    Resolving conflict in marriage / Darrell Hines.
        p. cm.
    ISBN 0-88368-729-1 (pbk. : alk. paper)
    1. Spouses—Religious life. 2. Marriage—Religious
    aspects—Christianity. 3. Conflict management—Religious
    aspects—Christianity. I. Title.
    BV4596.M3 H56 2002
    248.8'44—dc21
                                        2002000019

2 3 4 5 6 7 8 9 10 11 12 13 14 / 10 09 08 07 06 05 04 03 02

Dedication

After twenty-two years of marriage, my wife, Pamela, is without question the love of my life.

Because of the life-changing Word of God, we are together today and have overcome much opposition within our marriage. We have victoriously walked hand in hand through some of life's toughest blows; and although the enemy endeavored to separate us, God's love continued to draw us closer.

I dedicate this book to Pamela because she has proven to me over and over again that her love for me is undying. Life without her is unimaginable; her sweet and tender disposition is something that I will never want to live without.

I love you, Pamela Megan Hines.

Your husband,
Darrell Lynn Hines

Contents

Introduction

Marriage in Crisis

❖❖❖

Marriages are under attack today. The vast majority of Americans seem to agree this is the case. People today don't have the same approach toward marriage that people had forty or fifty years ago. A half century ago, divorce wasn't an "option" in the church. People stayed married no matter how bad things got in the relationship.

Today, people seem to have a "take a number" mind-set: "next"…"next"…"next." Some people go through spouses like they go through old pairs of shoes.

A half century ago, nobody had heard about prenuptial agreements. Nowadays, many people are making such agreements, and most say as they do, "This is just in case the marriage doesn't work out." There's an anticipation—even if it is largely unconscious—that the marriage will fail. The commitment going into the marriage is shaky.

Certainly there's good reason for these feelings. Nearly half of all marriages do end in divorce. Many live with severe conflict in their marriages. And very few people know what to do.

This book takes an approach that goes against the trends of the time:

• Marriage is God's idea, and therefore marriage must be held in high esteem.

• Conflict in marriage *can* be resolved.

- People can live in satisfying, fulfilling, long-standing marriages.

Conflicts *Can* Be Resolved

We each want to individualize our marital problems. We want to say, "Nobody has pain like I have pain. Nobody else has a problem as severe as my problem. Nobody else has a spouse who is quite as bad as my spouse."

Stop your excuses. Get honest with yourself and with God's Word.

God deals with us as individuals, but before He individualizes timing and specific methodology for our situation, He insists that we conform to His principles—and they do not change. God's principles for marriage are absolute and universal. They apply to everybody—to all marriages in all cultures at all times, regardless of individual situations, circumstances, or personalities.

God's principles for marriage are absolute and universal.

People come to the day of their wedding in many different ways. Some of those ways are cultural; some are personal.

In some cultures, people marry because they fall in love with each other and choose to marry.

In some cultures, people marry because their parents arranged the marriage. The arrangement may be rooted in social reasons, financial reasons, or religious reasons, or it simply might be a matter of "availability" or "intuition" on the part of the parents that the match is a good one.

In some cultures, a mixture of these two approaches is the custom—a couple may fall in love but not marry until (or unless) the parents give full agreement.

At times, of course, some couples marry because they have a baby prior to their wedding.

Regardless of the reasons or the path that brings two people together to a wedding day, the principles are the same for a couple to stay together in a marriage relationship that is mutually benefi-cial and satisfying.

God prepared the success of your marriage long before you ever got married. He set out the plan that would allow you to be happily, joyfully, and successfully married. Your part is to walk out God's plan. It's as you walk out *His* plan and not your own plan that your marriage takes on a deeper meaning and a deeper joy. It's then that marriage becomes truly satisfying and fulfilling.

> God prepared the success of your marriage long before you got married.

What is God's plan and purpose for your marriage? We turn there first....

1

God's Divine Plan for Your Marriage

❖❖❖

God saw everything that He had made, and indeed it was very good.
—Genesis 1:31

Marriages in our nation are failing at a rate of one out of two. One of the main reasons for our high divorce rate, in my opinion, is that married people do not know the reason for their marriage. They have never gone to God's Word and asked the question, "How does God see my marriage?"

Most people marry for selfish reasons. They want to be married because they believe marriage will satisfy some need in their lives. They want the security of marriage, the sexual pleasure of marriage, the companionship of marriage, the children who are born to marriage, and the happiness they believe to be associated with marriage. Again, we need to ask, "What is *God's* purpose for a man and a woman to be married?"

For the answer, we need to go to the book of Genesis. That's the book of beginning, the book of "seed," the book that gives us God's ideal. What the first Adam lost through his rebellion and sin, the Second Adam, Jesus Christ, regained for those who believe in Him and follow Him. We need to discover what was lost and what we can regain through faith in Jesus Christ.

God's Plan for God's Creation

From the very beginning of creation, marriage was not man's idea. It was God's idea. In the first chapter of Genesis we read this:

> Then God said, "Let Us make man in Our image, according to Our likeness; let them have dominion over the fish of the sea, over the birds of the air, and over the cattle, over all the earth and over every creeping thing that creeps on the earth." So God created man in His own image; in the image of God He created him; male and female He created them. Then God blessed them, and God said to them, "Be fruitful and multiply; fill the earth and the subdue it; have dominion over the fish of the sea, over the birds of the air, and over every living thing that moves on the earth."
>
> (Genesis 1:26–28)

These verses introduce to us the cornerstone of mankind's nature: the image of God. For anything to be successful and fruitful on this earth, it must be in the image of God.

In these verses, God—as a singular God—says, *"Let Us make man in Our image"*—plural. At this all-important beginning point, God displays the "community" aspect of our nature and God's nature. God exists as God the Father, God the Son, and God the Spirit. God exists as one entity with three functional representations. God is three, yet "one." God makes mankind *"male and female"*—two functional identities bound together as one. God created within the entity of "one" mankind a two-part being who is to live in harmony. God, as the Divine Family, created the human family in His image—separate functional representations of one entity.

In the institution of marriage, therefore, we see the reflection of God's image. Two become one.

One of the reasons the devil is so intent upon destroying marriages is that every time he sees a marriage in which two people truly have become one entity, the devil sees a reflection of God's nature. He sees unity, harmony, and oneness—a completely whole image of love and purpose.

We rarely approach marriage thinking that it is a reflection of God's image. A woman thinks, *I'm going to get myself a man to support me.* A man thinks, *I'm going to get myself a woman to cook and clean for me.* We never think, *We together will reflect God's image. That's the ultimate purpose for our marriage.* The result of our failure to think this way about our marriage is a casualness toward marriage, a disregard for the deep spiritual purpose for marriage, and oftentimes a quick justification for dissolving *"what God has joined together"* (Matthew 19:6).

Everywhere I look, I see patterns of marriage that are reflections of just about anything *but* God's nature.

Ask yourself today: "Does my marriage reflect God's nature? Or does it reflect the devil's nature?"

Let me assure you of this: The things in your marriage that are not like God will be the things that bother you the most. And those things that are like God—in you as a person, in your spouse as a person, in your relationship as a married couple—will be things that are blessings and that cause you to be a blessing to others. You won't have any problem with those things that are like God. The character traits, the behaviors, and the disharmony in relationship that are not like God will be what gnaws at you deep within your heart. Those will be the things that frustrate you, trouble your mind, and cause you to feel anger and anxiety.

The devil will always try to exaggerate that part of you that is not like God. He will seek to exaggerate any aspect of your marriage that is not like God because the devil knows that if he can turn your mind toward the ways you are not like God and can amplify those behaviors and traits, he will have started the process of *division.* He will have driven a wedge to divide you from God and to divide you from your spouse.

A Reflection of God's Nature

God created man to be like Himself. Being "in His image" means that man is to reflect God's nature. Certainly God is a spirit and we are flesh, but in our spirits and souls, we are created to be a reflection of God's spirit and soul. Mankind—which includes male and female—was created to think as God thought, speak as God spoke, act as God acted, feel as God felt, be motivated as God was motivated, and create as God created. The impulses of mankind's inner self—the dreams, desires, hopes, and love of men and women—were initially designed to reflect the way God dreams, what God desires and hopes, and the way God loves.

That is an awesome truth you need to ponder for a while in your heart. Let it fill your being. You as a human being were initially created in God's plan and purpose to reflect the nature of a holy God.

The Nature of God in "Relationship"

Father, Son, and Holy Spirit dwell in perfect harmony. Their relationship is perfect; they are united, totally in sync with one another to the point that they cannot be identified as separate in nature. They are separate only in *function*.

How does this relate to your marriage? God created you and your spouse to be joined together in a way that is totally united, in sync, and undifferentiated when it comes to your "nature" as married people. You and your spouse have separate *functions* in the marriage. You are of different sexes. You have different personalities and gifts and talents. But you are to be of one "nature" when it comes to your character, your commitment, and your Christlikeness. You are to be holy as God is holy. You are to reflect His nature of perfect communion with each other; you are to establish a perfect relationship marked by a perfect love, a perfect trust, a perfect communication.

Now this is God's ideal. None of us ever lives up to God's perfection or God's ideal, but this is what we are to seek to establish. It's how we are to seek to live. It's the goal at which we are to aim our lives and our marriages. This ideal about marriage is what God planned, what He desires, and what He is committed to helping you create.

A Sacred Bond

Throughout the Creation story in the Bible, we find one statement made repeatedly: *"And God saw that it was good."* But then we come to a verse in the second chapter of Genesis in which God says, *"It is not good"* (v. 18).

God looked and saw Adam tending the Garden of Eden and naming all the animals. Yet there was no helper or mate for Adam. There was nobody who was *"a helper comparable to him."* God said, *"It is not good that man should be alone; I will make him a helper comparable to him"* (v. 18).

So God caused a deep sleep to come on Adam, and He took one of his ribs and used it to form a woman. He closed up the wound in Adam's side, and after He had formed woman, He brought her to Adam, who said, *"This is now bone of my bones and flesh of my flesh; she shall be called Woman, because she was taken out of Man"* (v. 23).

Then God said, in response to this new creature of His making and the new relationship that was to exist between man and woman, *"Therefore a man shall leave his father and mother and be joined to his wife, and they shall become one flesh"* (v. 24).

God designed Adam and Eve to be together as one flesh. They were to be joined—not only for a brief period to make children, as was true for the other creatures of the Garden, but also in a lasting relationship. They were to become and remain *"one flesh."*

The word *holy* means to be "separate." God is holy; He is not like man. He is separate, above, infinite, and unfathomable in His power and wisdom and glory. He is too great and magnificent for our full comprehension. He is of a different order than mankind.

In the same way, mankind was to be "separate"—not like the animals but like God. We are to function on a higher level than biology. We are to live in the spirit as well as in the flesh. The bond of marriage is not for sex and procreation alone; it is a bond that is "holy," a bond that is separate from other physical creatures, a bond that has a sacred mark of approval upon it.

We are to function on a higher level than biology.

Not only were Adam and Eve made in the likeness of God—designed for community and the togetherness of a family—but they also were made with the enduring likeness of God who enters into relationship with mankind and never leaves that relationship. As we become one in spirit with the Lord through salvation, so man becomes one in flesh with a spouse through marriage.

Family Is Rooted in the Name of Jesus

The apostle Paul wrote to the Ephesians,

> *For this reason I bow my knees to the Father of our Lord Jesus Christ, from whom the whole family in heaven and earth is named, that He would grant you, according to the riches of His glory, to be strengthened with might through His Spirit in the inner man, that Christ may dwell in your hearts through faith; that you, being rooted and grounded in love, may be able to comprehend with all the saints what is the width and length and depth and height; to know the love of Christ which passes knowledge; that you may be filled with all the fullness of God.* (Ephesians 3:14–19)

Family is a word that is rooted in a name. We tend to think of family in terms of our surname—for example, Smith, Brown, or Hines. The Bible, however, tells us that family ultimately is rooted in the name of Jesus Christ. He is the One who defines family.

God is our Father.

God is Husband to His people.

God is like a nurturing mother.

Jesus is the Bridegroom.

The church is the bride.

The Bible is filled with images and references related to family. The family is God's idea, God's purpose and plan, the expression of His image!

What God defines, God supports. God provides for what He defines. God is the One who imparts to "family" all that "family" needs in order to survive: faith to believe in the love of God that is beyond measure.

God loves you...and He loves your marriage.

God blesses those whom He loves. He has spiritual and natural riches beyond measure for you...and for your marriage.

God has a purpose for those whom He loves. He has a purpose for you...and for your marriage.

What you need is the faith to believe in the love of God for yourself and your marriage! It is the challenge of your faith to believe for the *"width and length and depth and height"* of all that Jesus Christ desires to impart to you.

What keeps us from grabbing hold of that faith in God's love and purpose for us? For some, thought patterns need to be renewed. In some, stubborn wills need to be yielded. In some, hearts need to be restored.

The Defining Characteristic of the Relationship: Mutual Love

What marks the relationship among the Godhead? Mutual love. Jesus said, *"For the Father loves the Son, and shows Him all things that He Himself does; and He will show Him greater works than these, that you may marvel"* (John 5:20). Jesus also said, *"That the world may know that I love the Father, and as the Father gave Me commandment, so I do"* (John 14:31). God loves Jesus. Jesus loves God.

> The strongest mutual love is one that is not only physical, sexual, and emotional, but also spiritual.

The strongest mutual love is one that is not only physical, sexual, and emotional, but also spiritual.

Order within the Relationship: A Line of Authority

God's model for the family order is given in verse 3 of 1 Corinthians 11: *"The head of every man is Christ, the head of woman is man, and the head of Christ is God."*

Just as God the Father is the head of Jesus Christ, and Jesus Christ is the One who sent the Holy Spirit, so the order for mankind in marriage is Christ is head of man, man is head of woman, and parents are the head of their children. This is the line of authority. If that line is broken or ignored, conflict is automatic. Keep the line as God established it, and peace has an opportunity to flourish. Break the line of authority, and problems cannot help but emerge.

We will explore this line of authority and order more closely in the next chapter, but in order to lay a conceptual foundation for our discussion of husbands and wives, we need to understand several key truths that are part of what God established *"in the beginning"* (Genesis 1:1).

A Divine Purpose: To Bear Fruit and Have Dominion

At the Creation, God created *"male and female,"* and we read in the first chapter of the Bible that God *"blessed them"* (vv. 27–28). God's blessing was twofold: be fruitful and have dominion.

From the beginning, both male and female were to be fruitful. They were to produce, create, administrate, generate, and originate. What they produced was to be ongoing and self-producing. What was created was to create in turn. What was generated was to continue to generate. Until when? Until the whole earth was filled with the goodness of their work. God said, *"Be fruitful and multiply; fill the earth"* (v. 28). This was not to be the work of men only or of women only. They were to be fruitful *together* and multiply *together* and fill the earth *together.*

From the beginning, both male and female were given dominion over this earth. There was no "dominion" of man over woman or woman over man. Male and female were to have dominion over God's creatures—those creatures with beaks and gills and feathers and fur and hooves and claws and scales! God said, *"Subdue it* [the earth]; *have dominion over the fish of the sea, over the birds of the air, and over every living thing that moves on the earth"* (Genesis 1:28).

To have dominion means to take authority over something. And with authority over something comes responsibility for that something. As a parent, for example, you have authority over your children, and, at the same time, you have responsibility for your children. You always have responsibility for those things over which you have authority.

To have dominion doesn't mean that you know everything by yourself or that you are capable of doing all things by yourself. It means that you are in relationship with God and, *through His revelation and insights imparted to you,* you know what you need to know to have authority over the things that God gives you authority over. Some of the knowledge that God will impart to you is knowledge about how others are to take part in the accomplishment of a task. Some of the knowledge is about timing, methods, priority setting, and the "limits" of your particular role in the accomplishment of a specific task or goal.

Two Roles from One Being

Initially, the Bible tells us that Adam, whose name literally means "mankind," was one entity. Then God caused a deep sleep to fall on Adam, and He took a rib from Adam and created a woman out of man. Adam said,

> *This is now bone of my bones and flesh of my flesh; she shall be called Woman, because she was taken out of Man.*
> (Genesis 2:23)

God pulled all the "female" out of Adam and turned that female part of his identity into Woman. The Hebrew word for *woman* in Genesis 2 also can be translated as *wife.* It literally means "man with a womb"—a wife capable of bearing a husband's child.

The Bible clearly reserves marriage for two people of the opposite sex. To be a husband, a person must be male. To be a wife, a person must be female. There is no provision whatsoever for two males to be husband and wife or for two females to have a husband and wife relationship. Marriage is for two people who are of opposite sex. The two *together* create one complete entity before God, or together they reflect the image of God.

Female...wife...mother.

Male...husband...father.

The roles in marriage are highly gender specific!

A female qualifies to be a wife. A wife, in turn, qualifies to be a mother. Certainly, a female can become a mother before she becomes a wife—but that is out of God's divine order.

Being a male qualifies a person to be a husband, and, in turn, being a husband qualifies a man to be a father. Before a male is a husband, he has no authority over *any* female. It is only after he is a husband that he has authority over a wife. In the same way, a male has no authority over children until he becomes husband and *father.*

The Bible clearly reserves marriage for two people of the opposite sex.

Gender Differences in Functional Relationship

Female and male are equals. They are equal in their command to be fruitful and to have dominion over the earth.

As female and male enter into a marriage relationship and take on the roles of husband and wife, they take on different but complementary roles. They take on different *functions* in the marriage. And any time you take on functions or tasks or work with another person, you will find that one person needs to take the lead and have the greater responsibility for the accomplishment of the work. This is true for large groups of people, small groups of people, and a "group" that has only two people in it. No two people can lead at the same time.

Certainly, two or more people can discuss an issue; two or more people can debate an issue; two or more people can offer opinions about an issue; two people can do work related to the accomplishment of a project—but one person needs to be in the "point" position of making a final decision and setting the direction of the work. The person who takes on that role is the person who has the authority over the work and the responsibility for it.

After the Fall in the Garden of Eden, Adam was cursed with a curse of work, or hard labor. As a husband, he was put into the point position. He was to provide for his wife, and in so doing, he was responsible for her. After the Fall, Eve, as a wife, was put in a "follower" position. God told Eve, *"Your desire shall be for your husband, and he shall rule over you"* (Genesis 3:16).

It was after the Fall that Adam actually gave a name to Eve. Prior to the Fall, she was "woman" or "wife." After the Fall, Adam named his wife Eve *"because she was the mother of all living"* (v. 20). As a mother, Eve was to know the curse of sorrow and pain in childbearing. In turn, Adam became a "father" to the children Eve bore.

Note that both Adam and Eve were created to be fruitful and have dominion. They were not created with the ability to be husband and wife or father and mother. They had to *learn* how to be good marriage partners and how to be good parents. They were created with an ability to have authority or to take the lead over animals, fish, birds, "creeping" creatures, and all the plants in the Garden. They had to learn what it meant to lead and follow in relationship one to the other.

Also note this. At no time do we find God saying that man is to rule over woman. A man is to have responsibility for and to have authority (or "rulership") over *his own wife and family.* That's where he functions as a husband. There is no place in God's Word where we find God saying that men are to dominate women or have rule over any female who comes walking down the street. A man is a husband to one wife only, and he has rulership or leadership in his relationship with that one wife.

Marriage Requires the Adoption of Roles

Many men and women try to live after they are married as if they are still single. I've heard men say, "I'll go where I want and do what I want." Not if you want to be in God's will, you won't. I've heard women say, "No husband is going to tell me what I can and cannot do." Yes, he will, if you want to be in God's will.

Once you are married, you give up certain rights to your own freedom and self-expression.

The apostle Paul wrote about this to the Corinthians:

He who is unmarried cares for the things of the Lord; how he may please the Lord. But he who is married cares about the things of the world; how he may please his wife. There is a difference between a wife and a virgin. The unmarried woman cares about the things of the Lord, that she may be holy both in body and in spirit. But she who is married cares about the things of the world; how she may please her husband. (1 Corinthians 7:32–34)

The unmarried woman is not in submission to a man. Her submission is totally to the Lord, and from Him she draws her ability to be fruitful and have dominion. The married woman submits her life to the Lord, but she also submits her life to her husband, and her "cares" become concerns about how she may please her husband.

A female has the choice to say "no" to the opportunity to be a wife. But when a female says "yes," she takes on the identity of a wife. She takes on the responsibilities and privileges that are a part of being a wife according to God's Word.

A male has the choice to say "no" to being married. But when a male takes a wife, he takes on the identity of a husband. He takes on the responsibilities and privileges that are a part of being a husband according to God's Word.

Marriage Requires Leaving and Cleaving

Marriage requires that both husband and wife "leave their parents" and "cleave"—or be joined—to their spouses. A husband is no longer subject to the authority of his parents; a wife is no longer subject to her parents. A new household is established—a new family is formed—at the time of a wedding.

A number of conflicts in marriage arise because one or both spouses hasn't really "left home." They've never really cut the ties that bind them to their parents. For a marriage to be successful, both husband and wife need to leave mother and father and place each other in the role of "first and foremost" in their lives.

If you are a parent, you need to anticipate this time of "leaving and cleaving" for your own sons and daughters. From the time you have your children, you need to start anticipating the day when your children will leave your home and create homes of their own. God's plan is that your children leave you and cleave to somebody else. When your child marries, your child needs to make his or her spouse

If you are married, accept the fact that you are married.

"number one." At the time of their wedding, your child changes his or her foremost allegiance from you as a parent to the spouse.

To cleave to a spouse means to tie yourself closely to that spouse. It means to be married in every sense of the word and to accept "married" as your new identity.

If you are married, accept the fact that you are married! You aren't alone. You can't live totally for yourself. You must factor another person into your life.

If you aren't married, then you have a choice. But if you choose to be married, then you must choose God's rules regarding marriage.

To cleave means to share one schedule, one agenda, one set of goals and dreams, one "life" with your chosen spouse.

When you were single and went off for thirteen weeks in a row to do evangelistic or missionary work...great. But when you marry, you no longer do that—not without the full consent and participation of your spouse.

When you were single and you devoted four weeks to fasting and prayer...wonderful. But when you marry, you no longer do that—not without the full approval of your spouse.

When you were single and you devoted yourself to ministry with a single-hearted devotion...fine. But when you marry, you no longer can do that—your spouse comes before your ministry.

The Lord does not give a call to any man or woman that will divide a marriage.

God will not call a man to preach in Kalamazoo and have his family become a zoo. God is a God of order, of priority, of responsibility, of authority, of goodness—and the number one place for your Christian ministry is at home. As Paul wrote to the Galatians,

"Let us do good to all, especially to those who are of the house-hold of faith" (Galatians 6:10). Where is that household of faith first established? In homes of faithful men and women. Paul was talking about the church, but where is the church to be mani-fested? In the home. You and your spouse and your children are a household of faith if you are serving God and making your daily lives an act of worship before Him.

Both Spouses: Ongoing Submission to God

A great deal is said about submission in marriage, but this foun-dational principle needs to be understood: both husband and wife are to be submitted to God.

Your first responsibility in your marriage is to God. What you will find, however, in submitting first to God is this: as you submit your life to God, you will be submitted to what God wants for you in your marriage.

The flesh never wants to submit. The flesh doesn't agree with God's truth. In fact, it rebels against God's truth. That's why faith is a must. A person must choose by faith to do things God's way.

You can't be a good husband or wife on your own strength. You need to have the Lord in your marriage. And in order to have the Lord in your marriage, you need to invite Him into it.

It takes as much submission to God and as much faith for a husband to love his wife as Christ loves the church, as it takes for a woman to respond to her husband as the church responds to Christ.

Submission and faith are required by both husbands and wives. The attitude of the heart must be to yield to God. The prevailing attitude must be to line up your life according to God's Word.

Submission doesn't work if only one person is submitted to doing things God's way. A husband has to submit to God's way; he has to submit to the plan and yield himself to becoming a husband who reflects Christ's love and provision. A wife has to submit to God's way. She has to yield to God first, so that she might be a wife who reflects the church's role as a loving, praising, submitted helpmate.

Both husband and wife must rebuke their own stubborn wills and choose to do things God's way—not the way that's defined on popular television talk shows or the way Aunt June Bug defines marriage. Are you willing to submit yourself to God's plan?

Both men and women need to understand that submission never reduces a person in God's eyes. Submission does not take away one bit of a person's potential or purpose. It doesn't diminish or reduce any of the gifts, talents, or skills a person has. Rather, submission puts a person into a position of obedience so God can use that person. When a wife submits to a husband, she is never "less" than her husband. Rather, she is fulfilling her role so that God can use her, use her husband, and use their marriage in a way that God desires.

When a man loves his wife and pours out himself to care for her, love her, protect and provide for her, and be available to her, he is not "less" than a man. Some husbands seem to think so. They think that if they give of themselves, they'll lose something. Whatever you give away of yourself, husband, God will grow back! He'll bless what you give. And in your giving, you are putting yourself, your wife, and your marriage into a position where God can use you and bless you in the way He desires.

What exactly does God desire? He desires for a married couple to reflect His nature on this earth, to be a witness to the saving grace of Jesus Christ, to raise up children in the Lord (both those to whom they give birth and those whom they lead to the Lord), and to be the recipients of His total blessing—physical, emotional, financial, material, and spiritual!

Isn't that what you want—for yourself, for your spouse, and for your children? The only way to receive this from God is to submit to doing things God's way! Your attitude toward God will determine your attitude toward your mate.

Both Spouses: Ongoing Service for God and to Each Other

Just as both husbands and wives are called to ongoing submission to God, so both husbands and wives are called to ongoing service for God and each other.

Your attitude toward God will determine your attitude toward your mate. Both husbands and wives are to continue ministering to the Lord and for the Lord. Both are to remain active in their witness to Christ Jesus as Savior and Lord. Both are to manifest the spiritual and natural gifts that God has given to them.

Husbands are called to serve their wives, just as Christ serves the church with His presence, protection, power, and provision. Christ laid down His life for the church. Husbands are called to lay down their pride and their selfishness to serve their wives.

Wives are called to serve their husbands, just as the church serves Christ with its praise, its practical service, its yielding to Christ's will, and its fulfillment of God's directives. Wives are called to lay down their pride and their selfishness to serve their husbands.

When we understand that both husbands and wives are to fill gender-specific roles, that they are called to ongoing submission to God, and that they are called to ongoing service to God and each other, then we have the proper God-ordained framework for truly understanding the roles prescribed for husbands and wives.

2

Husbands and Wives

❧❦

Wives, submit to your own husbands, as is fitting in the Lord.
Husbands, love your wives and do not be bitter toward them.
—Colossians 3:18–19

What model for relating to your husband or wife are you following? For most people, the model they follow is the model they saw in their mothers and fathers. For many, it is what the "culture" says a marriage should look like. The Christian, however, has a model that is God-given. It is a model of the way Jesus loves the church and the church submits to Jesus.

"But I wasn't a Christian when I got married."

Are you a Christian now? If you are, then you need to start lining up your marriage and your role in that marriage to follow God's Word. It might not be the way you have functioned as a husband or wife in the past, but it's the way God calls you to function as a husband or wife now. Start today.

The apostle Paul described the functional pattern for husbands and wives in a letter he wrote to the early Christians in Ephesus:

Wives, submit to your own husbands, as to the Lord. For the husband is head of the wife, as also Christ is head of the church; and He is the Savior of the body. Therefore, just as the church is subject to Christ, so let the wives be to their own husbands in everything. Husbands, love your wives, just as Christ also loved the church and gave Himself for her, that He might sanctify and cleanse her with the washing of water by the word, that He might present her to Himself a glorious church, not having spot or wrinkle or any such thing, but that she should be holy and without blemish. So husbands ought to love their own wives as their own bodies; he who loves his wife loves himself. For no one ever hated his own flesh, but nourishes and cherishes it, just as the Lord does the church. For we are members of His body, of His flesh and of His bones. "For this reason a man shall leave his father and mother and be joined to his wife, and the two shall become one flesh." This is a great mystery, but I speak concerning Christ and the church. Nevertheless let each one of you in particular so love his own wife as himself, and let the wife see that she respects her husband. (Ephesians 5:22–33)

This model for marriage—based upon the heavenly reality of the way Jesus Christ relates to His church—is how marriage is intended to look. It's how marriage is intended to function.

The Role of the Godly Husband

Early in my ministry, I traveled a great deal. My wife, Pamela, was left at home with our two sons. She was totally responsible for getting our sons to school, taking one of them to therapy every day for treatment of his cerebral palsy, and keeping the house going—by herself. I was all over the country, preaching and teaching, while she was paying the bills, dealing with a broken-down car, and getting the groceries.

I came home from one evangelistic trip, and Pam said, "Honey, I need a man."

I was startled. My first thought, of course, was that she needed sexual gratification. That wasn't at all what she meant. She needed a man at home—a man she could talk to, a man who would help carry part of the load, a man who would be there for her.

I decided I was that man! I made a decision to stay home more, to take her on the road with me more, to help out more with our boys. I wasn't about to have my beautiful twenty-something-year-old wife needing a "man" while I was away from home. I wasn't about to give the devil that open door into our marriage.

My first response could have been, "You've got a man. What do you think I am, a boy? Are you calling me a boy? I'm your man."

Rather, I sacrificed a little of my pride and admitted that I hadn't been there for my wife in all the ways a husband and father should be there for his family. I decided that I would be the head of my family not just when I happened to be at home, but all the time. I decided that I would pattern my role as a husband on the way the Bible described it—I would be for my wife a reflection of the way Jesus related to the church.

Husband, how are you going to look like Jesus in your marriage? That's the key question for you to ask.

First, you need to look to Christ as the Divine Bridegroom. Learn how He relates to the church. You'll find that Jesus loves the church. He sacrifices for the church. He listens to the concerns of the church. He provides for the church and takes care of the church. He is sensitive to the needs and hurts of the church. Furthermore, Jesus loves and relates to the church *as His own body.* In fact, another term for the church is the "body of Christ."

This is the challenge to a husband: love your wife as you love your own self. Begin to give to your wife, listen to your wife, provide for your wife, and be sensitive to your wife as Jesus is sensitive to the church.

"But she...," husbands say. Husbands always seem to have a response. "But, pastor, you don't understand. My wife is nothing like the church." Adam said a similar thing. "This woman You gave me...." (See Genesis 3:12.) Husbands have been blaming their wives for their own failures since the very beginning!

Husband, stop blaming your wife for your lack of relating to her as Christ relates to the church.

Jesus could say a similar thing: "This church—this 'body' of Mine—is nothing like Me." But Jesus doesn't take that approach. Jesus loves the church just as the church is. Jesus sacrificed for the church *"while we were still sinners"* (Romans 5:8). Jesus doesn't wait for the church to become perfect before He loves the church, gives to the church, provides for the church, or cares for the church. Jesus loves the church, period.

Husband, your responsibility to your wife has nothing to do with the character or behavior of your wife. It has everything to do with the character of God. It has everything to do with how you will choose to reflect the nature of Jesus Christ. It has everything to do with how you begin to reflect the nature of God.

Your becoming a reflection of Jesus has nothing to do with your own ability and strength. You must have the grace of God working in you and flowing through you to reflect Jesus. The Bible says,

> *For by grace you have been saved through faith, and that not of yourselves; it is the gift of God, not of works, lest anyone should boast. For we are His workmanship, created in Christ Jesus for good works, which God prepared beforehand that we should walk in them.* (Ephesians 2:8–10)

Marriage is not designed to work by your human effort alone. It is designed to work as you allow the nature of Christ to be manifested in you and through you. It is intended to function with God's help, God's direction, and God's grace.

When you become irritated or frustrated or discouraged about the way things are in your marriage, don't respond out of your fleshly weakness. Go to God! Pray for your wife and your marriage. Fast and pray, if necessary. Get into God's Word. Renew your mind with the way God would have you think and respond to your wife. Ask God to help you speak to your wife as He would have you speak to her. Ask God to help you act toward your wife as He would have you act toward her.

Marriage is not designed to work by human effort alone.

This is something you do regardless of how your wife responds or acts or reacts.

The Bible gives us this teaching for husbands:

Husbands...dwell with them [your wives] *with understanding, giving honor to the wife, as to the weaker vessel, and as being heirs together of the grace of life, that your prayers may not be hindered.* (1 Peter 3:7)

Let's take a closer look at several key phrases in this passage.

Weaker Vessel

Husbands are to honor their wives as the *"weaker vessel."* This does not mean that the husband has more ability, intelligence, or spiritual gifts than his wife. It means that he has the responsibility to honor her with his strength. What is a husband's strength? It is his ability to provide for his wife and protect his wife.

The husband is given the responsibility for providing materially and physically for his wife and for protecting her from harm as part of his having authority over her. Protecting your wife means protecting her from starvation, nakedness, shame, spiritual attack, physical assault, and poverty. Name anything that can destroy or diminish a person, and that is something from which a husband has the responsibility to protect his wife.

Husband, get an understanding about your wife's strengths and limitations. Don't press her beyond what she is capable of doing or what she desires to do. Do encourage her to use and develop her strengths.

A husband is expected to be a protector and provider, not an abuser or a user.

A husband should be a "requester," not a "demander."

A husband should be a "husband" and not a "master." (See Hosea 2:16.)

Keep in mind always that "weaker" does not mean "less spiritual." God does not give more of Himself to you because you are a man or because you are a husband. Nor does it mean that in giving you more, He gives your wife less because she is a woman or a wife. In Christ, there is no male or female. You are "one" in Christ Jesus—which means "equal" before the Lord in the gift of salvation, in the impartation and ministration of the gifts of the

Holy Spirit, and in opportunities for spiritual growth and conformation to the likeness of Christ Jesus. (See Galatians 3:28.)

Honor Your Wife

Peter calls husbands to "honor their wives." What does it mean to honor someone? It means to hold that person in your mind and heart as God holds that person. It means to see a person as God sees that person. In the case of your wife who is a believer, it means getting a picture of how God wants to use her in His kingdom. It means seeing your wife as a person who is loved by God, born again, filled with the Spirit, operating in spiritual gifts, and fulfilling a ministry role on this earth. It means seeing your wife as a person who is gifted, capable, talented, and blessed—a woman who has been given specific abilities and capacities by God her Creator. It means seeing your wife as someone to be respected and held in esteem. It means seeing your wife as a person you are to treat with kindness, mercy, generosity, patience, and, at all times, love.

Jesus never exploits the submission of the church. He responds to submission with blessing and the outpouring of Himself. Husbands, you are challenged to do the same. You are never to exploit the submission of your wife and turn her into your slave or dominate her and attempt to control her against her will. Rather, you are to respond to her submission with an outpouring of yourself—a total giving. You are to be available to your spouse, communicate with your spouse, love your spouse, and be tender to your spouse. That's the way Jesus treats the church.

Joint-heirs of Grace

Peter called husbands to see themselves and their wives as being heirs together of *"the grace of life."* What God imparts to one, God imparts to both. Both husband and wife are heirs of God's grace. They are heirs of God's inheritance and prosperity—in spirit, mind, and body. They are heirs of God's call on their *life together as one flesh* to pursue the ministry that God has for them *as a couple.*

Grace is God's work manifested in our lives. It is His work in us, through us, for us, and all around us. As husband and wife you are joint-heirs of God's work. He isn't going to do something in you that He doesn't also desire to do in your wife. He isn't going to call you to do something without calling your wife to be by your side in fulfilling that call. Now, you may need to travel some, and your wife may need to stay at home with the children some—or, in other cases, all of you may need to be on the road together for the Lord—but the plan of God is that you are both called to *one ministry together.* God isn't going to require something of you without also requiring it of your wife. He isn't going to prepare you for a ministry without also making a plan and provision for the preparation of your wife. He isn't going to give you opportunities without factoring your wife into those opportunities.

Husband, don't exclude your wife from your ministry. Factor her into it!

I am blessed because my wife is a woman of prayer. I am blessed because my wife hears from God. I am blessed by every sermon my wife preaches. She is a joint-heir of God's grace with me!

Unhindered Prayers

Peter told husbands that they needed to dwell with their wives with understanding, give honor to their wives, and see themselves as being heirs together with their wives...to what end? So their prayers would not be hindered. (See 1 Peter 3:7.)

Husband, God will not hear a prayer that is a request for Him to do something in your life alone; rather, He will hear your prayers that are requests for God to do something in your life as a married man. He will hear your prayers that are petitions for Him to act in a way that brings blessing not only to you, but also to your wife and your family as a whole.

Husband, God will not hear a prayer that exalts you and brings disrepute to your wife. Rather, He will hear a prayer that builds up your marriage and that builds up your spouse.

Husband, God will not hear your prayers if those prayers are contradictory to His Word. He will not hear you if you are acting in disobedience to Him, including disobedience in your marriage.

Rather, He will hear your prayers that are voiced in humble obedience and yielding to His commandments.

The Function of a Godly Wife

Wife, how are you going to look like the church in your marriage? That's the key question for you to ask.

Your behavior toward your husband has nothing to do with how your husband treats you. That's a difficult truth for many women to swallow, but it's the truth nonetheless.

Your marriage will be successful only if you are willing to treat your husband as God directs you to treat your husband, and not according to what your husband "deserves" or what you think he deserves.

Take a look at the chosen bride of Christ, the church. *"Just as the church is subject to Christ, so let the wives be to their own husbands in everything"* (Ephesians 5:24).

How does the church relate to Christ Jesus?

The church respects Christ. It acknowledges Him as the Head of the body, the Head of the family of God. It responds to His leadership by doing what He needs and wants done. It listens to Him. It praises Him. It lines up its purpose and will with His purpose and will so there's a unity of purpose and will. It seeks to become a true helper in fulfilling His mission on this earth.

Wife, that's your challenge. Show respect to your husband. Acknowledge that he is the head of your marriage and your family. Respond to his leadership—find out what he needs and wants done and do that. Listen to him. Praise him and appreciate him. Line up with what he perceives to be the purpose and will of God for your marriage and family. Seek to become a true helper so that together the two of you can fulfill the mission God has for you on this earth.

A wife has an effect on her husband that no other person has. A wife has an ability to influence her husband like no other person can. A wife can build up her husband and help her husband in ways nobody else can. And, to the contrary, she also has an ability to hurt him, destroy his work, and distract him from what he needs to be doing as no other person can.

Submission doesn't mean that a wife loses "power."

To the contrary, a wife who is submissive to her husband has great influence on her husband. She has tremendous ability to give him strength, to build him up, to establish his reputation in the community, and to keep him in right standing with the Lord.

A wife has the ability to build up or tear down her household—which includes her husband and her children. By her words and deeds, she can help her husband find his calling from God and his purpose for living and then pursue that call and fulfill his purpose. Or she can keep him from doing what God created him to be and do.

A wife has the ability to create an environment that is so appealing that her husband can hardly wait to get home! Show me a wife who greets her husband looking her best and with a positive attitude...show me a wife who prepares for her husband a clean home and a good meal at the end of a day...show me a wife who has her children behaving and eager to see their father—and I'll show you a husband who can hardly wait to get home. It doesn't matter what kind of day he's had; if his wife is waiting for him with open arms and an encouraging word, he feels loved and appreciated and invigorated to have a better day tomorrow.

Every Wife Is a "Minister"

Every wife is in ministry—she is first and foremost a minister to her husband. Being submitted is a key factor in her ability to minister.

The Greek word for "submission" is actually made up of two words—one means "under," and the other means "to arrange in an orderly manner." A person who submits is a person who puts him- or herself under God's arranged order. You may need to tell yourself a dozen times a day, "God, I will stay in Your order. I will not treat my spouse the way I want to treat my spouse—I will treat my spouse the way You want me to treat my spouse. I will stay in Your order, I will stay in Your order, I will stay in Your order."

To submit, therefore, means to be the supportive part of a two-person union. Wives are not inferior to their husbands. That's like saying a person's body is inferior to that person's head. Wives complement their husbands; they are the second half of their husbands—the half that stands beside him, supports him, and helps him in all that he determines the two of you do together.

An Act of Faith

Wives don't submit to their husbands because they want to submit—in fact, in many cases they don't want to submit. They submit to their husbands because God commands it. Submission is *"as to the Lord"* (Ephesians 5:22).

Submission is not an automatic response for a woman. In fact, it is a response that goes against the way a woman is created as a woman. Submission, however, is what is required for women who are wives.

When God requires something of us, He always promises to help us do it. I've had many women tell my wife and I in marriage counseling, "I just can't submit. You don't know the man you are asking me to submit to." No, I don't. But God does. And God has put you in a marriage. If you want that marriage to work—I mean really work the way God means for it to work—you will have to do things God's way. As you submit as an act of your faith, God responds to your faithful submission, and the results of your submission are up to God. In submitting to your husband, you have just given God direct permission to work on your husband. As long as you get your will in the way as a wife, your husband will respond to you and not God. But when you submit, your husband has no interference. He's in a direct line for God to deal with him.

A woman submits herself to her own husband. To do that, you have to know what your husband needs. You have to learn what your husband wants, the praise your husband needs, the dreams your husband has, and the direction your husband is moving.

The Bible says, *"Whatever you do in word or deed, do all in the name of the Lord Jesus, giving thanks to God the Father through Him"* (Colossians 3:17).

Submission Is Not Conditional

Many women choose to submit only when they like the outcome they get from their submission. It's easy to submit when a husband is loving and kind, there's money in the bank, the children are well-behaved, and things in the bedroom are going well. It's easy to submit to a husband "as long as..."—and you can fill in that blank with whatever conditions you are holding over your husband. Wives who say, "I'll submit as long as..." already have an exit plan in place for what it will take for them to leave their husbands. That's not genuine submission; that's the exact opposite of submission. It's just biding your time until the divorce and, in the meantime, using submission as a means of manipulating your husband so you will get your way.

A woman once said to me, "Are you telling me, Pastor, that I need to submit to my husband even though he doesn't know God?"

I said simply, "That's what you agreed to do when you married him."

"But he's not saved. I'm supposed to submit to him when he's not saved?"

"He wasn't saved when you married him. Why did you agree to submit to a man who wasn't saved? His lack of salvation is a problem—I'm not disagreeing with you on that point. But your lack of submission is also a problem—and that's the problem that you can deal with. His salvation and your lack of submission are both problems to God. The one area in which you and God can work something out to your benefit is the area in which you alone are responsible—and that's the area of your submission."

An Expression of Your Witness

Submission is an extremely valuable expression of a wife's witness for Christ. God's Word says this:

> Wives...be submissive to your own husbands, that even if some do not obey the word, they, without a word, may be won by the conduct of their wives, when they observe your chaste conduct accompanied by fear [of God]. Do not

let your adornment be merely outward; arranging the hair, wearing gold, or putting on fine apparel; rather let it be the hidden person of the heart, with the incorruptible beauty of a gentle and quiet spirit, which is very precious in the sight of God. For in this manner, in former times, the holy women who trusted in God also adorned themselves, being submissive to their own husbands, as Sarah obeyed Abraham, calling him lord, whose daughters you are if you do good and are not afraid with any terror. (1 Peter 3:1–6)

A quiet, meek, humble spirit before your husband will do more to influence your husband toward God than all the sermons you could ever preach or all the nagging you could ever do.

Let me also say this to you who may be single: if you don't want to submit to the man you are planning to marry, don't marry him. Submission is an inescapable part of God's plan for marriage.

Spiritual Strength in Submission

The fact is, there is great spiritual strength in being submitted. The greatest strength is this—you are putting yourself into a position to be blessed. God will honor what you do and reward you. Every need you have as a woman and as a wife will be met by God in the way that you need that need to be met. God will work on your husband to bring him to the place where he starts being the husband God desires him to be—which is a husband you want. God will cause him to love you, honor you, respect you, provide for you, and be the sheltering, protecting "covering" over your life. Until that day, God will pour His love into your heart, and He will meet your needs.

> There is great spiritual strength in being submitted.

The opposite principle is also true—there is great weakness in being a nagging, domineering wife. Your husband will reject you, dismiss you, walk away from you, and sooner or later, stop loving you and caring about being married to you. The greatest weakness, however, is that you will be out of position to be blessed directly by God.

Both Husband and Wife Must Submit

"Submitting" must always be understood in the context that both husband and wife in a marriage are submitted to God.

Let me repeat: The flesh never wants to submit. That's why you need faith. It takes faith to choose to do things God's way.

A husband needs just as much faith and submission to God to love his wife as Christ loves the church, as a woman needs faith and submission to God to respond to her husband as the church responds to Christ.

Again, both husbands and wives need submission and faith. Your heart attitude must be one of yieldedness to God. Your primary goal should be to line up your life according to God's Word.

3

Agree to Agree

Six Foundation Stones of Agreement

❖❖❖

Can two walk together, unless they are agreed?
—Amos 3:3

At the heart of conflict is "disagreement"—a failure to agree. Agreement is the way that a husband and wife become *one* in flesh. One Word of God, one agreement, one vow, one set of principles on which the marriage functions, one spouse loved in faithfulness.

I have yet to see a marriage "endure with joy" without these six basic foundation stones of agreement in place:

- An agreement to build the marriage on God's Word.
- An agreement to leave the past behind.
- An ongoing agreement to "work" on the marriage.
- An agreement that both husband and wife need to "change."
- An agreement to disagree.
- An agreement to give 100 percent.

Let's take a look at each of these agreements more closely.

An Agreement to Build the Marriage on God's Word

My wife, Pam, and I came to our marriage with two different backgrounds and teachings about marriage. Pam grew up in a home in which the women "bailed out" if the pressure got too great in a relationship. I grew up in a home in which the men remained in their marriages no matter what happened, but they also dominated their women. The women in my family did what their husbands told them to do. After seven years of marriage, our two "backgrounds" clashed!

I was trying to dominate Pam. What she had to say wasn't important to me. She was struggling under the pressure of my domineering ways. We loved each other desperately, and we both wanted to have a happy marriage—but something wasn't working. We were operating according to two different sets of rules regarding marriage, and neither one of them was completely biblical.

We made a decision to wipe the slate clean, go to God's Word and learn from it, and give up anything in our behavior or attitude that was contrary to God's Word. We made a deal: "I will treat you the way the Bible tells me to treat you, and whatever I have to do to make that happen, I'm willing to do it."

From that moment, we began to work on ourselves.

If you will make the Word of God your focus, if you will read it together and make a mutual decision that you will do what it says, you won't need twenty marriage counselors. You will have one Marriage Counselor.

If you will make a decision to do what the Bible tells you to do, the focus will be on yourself and on your fulfilling or not fulfilling your proper God-given role as a husband or wife, rather than on what your spouse is or isn't doing.

Make a decision to do what the Bible says to do.

Make a decision to do what the Bible says to do from this day until the day you die or the day Jesus comes. Don't turn to the left or right, regardless of what other people say to you.

An Agreement to Leave the Past Behind

The principles of marriage are not altered on the basis of our previous experiences. Even though you were hurt, abused, or rejected in the past, you don't have any special privileges to set aside any of the requirements of marriage. As a wife, you are still to submit to your husband. As a husband, you are still to love your wife with a sacrificial, self-giving love.

Your previous relationships do not dictate what you will and won't do in marriage.

Time and again, I see people struggling in their marriages because they are comparing their spouse to that "perfect" person they think they dated for two months while they were in high school. Or they are comparing the way their spouse does or doesn't treat them to the way they were treated by someone in the past. Even worse, some are *anticipating* that their spouse will mistreat them or abuse them in the way a person mistreated or abused them in the past. They are living with a sense of dread and fear, just waiting for the day when their spouse erupts in anger, falls into a sullen silence, or walks away and doesn't come back.

Separate yourself from expectations based upon past performance and behavior. Choose to believe for a godly relationship based upon godly principles. Choose to be a godly person in the marriage relationship; choose to do things God's way. Then, anticipate that your spouse also will choose to be a godly person who will do things God's way.

Separate yourself from expectations based upon past performance and behavior.

Those who live in fear or dread, as well as those who live in a constant state of comparison, never find genuine happiness with the person who is in the "now" of their lives. They are always looking over their shoulders at what once was, or they are looking to the side to see what "might be" or "might have been" with another person.

I once heard about a woman whose father was an adulterous, unfaithful man. He had left this woman's mother at least five or six times to live with other women. Each time he came back, but he never stayed for longer than a year or two before he wandered off again. This woman married a man who was not at all like her father. Although her husband was 100 percent faithful to her, she seemed to do everything she could think of to test his faithfulness. Would he leave her if she overspent their budget? Would he leave her if she flirted with another man? Would he leave her if she mistreated him? He stayed faithful.

Twenty-five years after they had married, she left him. She told a counselor, "For twenty-five years I've lived with the dread that my husband would walk out on me and choose another woman. I just can't live in that fear and anxiety any longer. I'm not going to stay around and wait for that day to arrive. I've got to get out."

Talk about irrational thinking and behavior! That's the most severe case I've encountered, but what I do see are many spouses who constantly "push the buttons" that they know will trigger anger or frustration or disappointment in their spouses just to test them, usually with this claim: "I just wanted to see if my spouse still loves me."

I had a man tell me one time, "I don't trust preachers."

"Why not?" I asked.

"I've heard a lot of preachers, and I just don't trust preachers."

"Have you ever heard me preach?"

"No," he said.

"Well, then," I said, "don't take that old baggage on this trip."

You owe it to your spouse—and you owe it to *yourself*—to leave old opinions about people in your old past in the old dust.

Assume your spouse means what he or she says. Give your spouse the benefit of the doubt. Don't keep anticipating that the "other shoe will drop." Assume instead that there is no other shoe!

An Agreement to "Work" on the Marriage

Some people believe that if two people love each other, they don't have to "work" at their relationship. Some believe that a relationship should be just a spontaneous, go-with-the-flow, act-on-your feelings phenomenon. Some people are wrong!

Marriage is just like any other relationship. In order for it to grow, develop, flourish, and be fruitful and productive, a marriage needs to receive care, attention, time, and nurturing.

Other people just simply aren't willing to work on their marriage.

They'll work on their car.

They'll work on their house.

They'll work on their career.

They'll work on their wardrobe.

They'll work at their ministry for the Lord.

They'll work out at the gym.

But they won't work on relationships.

In the end, relationships are the only eternal thing worth working on! We always need to be working on our relationship with the Lord. We always need to be working on our relationship with our spouse and other family members entrusted to our care and responsibility. We always need to be working on our relationships with friends and those

> Relationships are the only eternal thing worth working on.

with whom we worship; after all, these fellow saints are going to be people we live with forever! We always need to be working on our relationships with people whom we are trying to influence for Christ.

What does it mean to work on a relationship?

It means you spend time talking to that person and being with that person. It means you make the effort to get to know the person—to know their likes and dislikes, their desires and their fears, their past accomplishments and their future goals. It means you spend some money—going on dates, having lunch or dinner together, spending some time at retreats together, and going on missions or evangelistic witnessing trips together. (Even if it's a trip around your neighborhood on foot, ringing doorbells of those who are unsaved and inviting them to church.) Working at a relationship means giving something of yourself that is sometimes difficult to give—giving up a little of your pride and self-centeredness to give part of yourself to another person.

Now, by working on the marriage I do *not* mean working on your spouse. Never marry somebody you intend to make over or to transform into the person you really want. It won't happen. You may influence a person for good and help a person become all that God created him or her to be, but you aren't going to change an old mule into a sleek racehorse.

The foremost work needs to be on yourself.

Your job is to work on *you*.

It's not your job to work on your spouse. That's God's job.

It's not your spouse's job to work on you.

It's *your* job to work on *you*.

God never holds you responsible for another person's salvation and righteousness. Neither does He hold another person responsible for your salvation and righteousness.

When I speak about working on the marriage, I am speaking about investing time, energy, and creativity into the marriage.

There are people who spend more time trying to figure out how to get out of their marriage than they have ever spent trying to figure out how to fix or improve their marriage!

People put more energy into buying cars, into doing their jobs, and even into building their wardrobes than they put into improving their marriages.

Agree with your spouse that you both will give serious time, attention, creative energy, and physical energy into ways you can improve your communication, your ministry together, your home life, your sexual life, your health, your finances and business relationships, your involvement in a church, your social life, and your spiritual life together as a couple.

An Agreement That You Both Need to Change

Growth is change. Becoming mature involves change. Development and multiplication involve change.

A marriage also requires change on the part of both the husband and wife. One person alone never is responsible for doing all the changing.

Go into marriage with an understanding that change is part of the package.

It isn't natural for a husband to love his wife as Christ loves the church. It isn't natural for a wife to submit to her husband as the church submits to Christ. Both husbands and wives need to change.

> Go into marriage with an understanding that change is part of the package.

Change means grabbing hold of your own stubborn will and laying it at the feet of Jesus.

Change means getting the counsel of God in areas where you don't know God's plan or aren't sure of God's purposes.

Change means getting rid of selfishness.

Change means taking charge of your attitude, your speech, your temper, and your behavior and putting every aspect of your life under the authority of God's Word.

Change may mean getting rid of some of your so-called friends.

Change means spending more time in prayer and fasting.

Change means spending more time in God's Word.

"But I can't change"…"I'm just the way I am"…"I'm too set in my ways"…"You can't change the spots on a leopard."

Those are lies from the devil. Furthermore, you aren't a leopard. The truth of God is that you *can* change your attitudes, your behavior, your habits, and the way you conduct your marriage.

A man said to me one time, "Every man in my family—from my great-grandfather to my grandfather to my father to my uncles to my brothers—has been married three times." He said this as if he was already making an excuse for leaving his present wife and moving on to wife number two, believing there was a wife number three in his future! That man needs to do some changing!

Most people actually know ways in which they personally need to change; they are just reluctant to admit the changes they know they need to make. Most people know which aspects of their personality and behavior aren't reflecting God. They may not want to admit what they know to other people, or even to themselves, but deep down inside, they know the ways in which they are not living up to God's ideal. That's an intuitive understanding that men and women have regardless of their culture, race, heritage, background, or religion. We have an inborn *knowing* that we are not living up to the perfection of God—we have an inborn knowing that we are sinners from our birth and that we have guilt wrapped around our souls.

The same is true for our marriages. Most people know which aspects of their functioning as a wife or a husband are unlike God's perfection. They just don't want to admit that they aren't acting like a godly husband or wife. In fact, people usually tend to point to the ways in which their spouse is acting in an ungodly manner, or the ways in which they believe their spouse is causing them to act ungodly.

"He just knows how to push my buttons." Ma'am, have you thought about removing some of those buttons from your life?

"She knows how to get under my skin." Sir, have you thought about how to speak to her and how to treat her so she has no reason to even try to get under your skin?

An Agreement to Disagree

Agreement doesn't necessarily mean that you do everything together or that you do everything alike. Total agreement is never possible because we all have our own unique likes and dislikes.

I once heard about a married couple who had been happily married for more than forty years. They both were strong Christians, but they did not go to the same church. The man was a Sunday school teacher and a deacon in one church. The woman was a faithful member of another church, where she was active in one of the women's groups. He liked an informal service; she liked a formal service. He liked singing choruses; she liked singing hymns. He liked long, teaching sermons. She liked short, inspirational sermons. He liked having an emphasis on the sermon; she liked having an emphasis on worship. He didn't feel a need for taking Communion more than once a month; she wanted to partake of the Lord's Supper every week.

Now were these two people in agreement about what they liked and disliked in this area of their relationship? No.

Did they ever find a common church home? No.

Did they have agreement? Yes—they *agreed to disagree.* They agreed to love and serve each other in Christ Jesus. They agreed that they would be Christians and that they would go to church on Sunday morning. They had agreement on basic doctrinal positions. They agreed at a deep level on matters of faith and devotion to the Lord—the issue of membership was a superficial issue to them.

You may like Mexican food, and your spouse may detest it. Your spouse may like Chinese food, and you may detest it.

You may like driving one kind of car; your spouse may enjoy driving another. In fact, if you look at any two-car family, you are going to find that, nine times out of ten, those two cars are different makes and models!

You may be a night person; your spouse may be a morning person.

Find areas of compromise and agreement within your differences. Don't expect your spouse to change everything to become a mirror image of your wants, your desires, your choices, your style, and your likes and dislikes. Value the differences you have, and seek agreement at deeper levels. It's more important that you eat together than that you eat the same food. It's more important that you travel down life's road together than that you ride in the same kind of vehicle. It's more important that you find times to communicate about your day than that you both have exactly the same waking and sleeping schedule.

> Value the differences you have, and seek agreement at deeper levels.

51

When my wife was pregnant with our second son, she developed a craving for a particular type of food. We went to her favorite restaurant for that type of food so much that I could hardly stand to see the commercials on television for that restaurant. By the time she delivered our son, I was sick of that place and everything on their menu!

My wife, however, continued to like that kind of food and that one particular restaurant. I had a choice: I could make this a big issue and drive a wedge between us in trying to get her to give up something she liked, or I could develop a liking for this kind of food and go along with her desire. I chose to do the latter.

I wanted "agreement" over the dinner table more than I wanted to have my own way.

There are times when you are wise to say, "I can bend and not break. I can adjust, adapt, be flexible, and go with my spouse's choice on this. It's not an ego issue for me—it's not a matter of control or pride." Agreement sometimes requires that we lay down our own foolish pride and let the other person have his or her "say" or his or her "way."

Many people believe marriage is a fifty-fifty arrangement. Not so!

Agreement is not defined as "my way or the highway." Agreement is not something that one spouse dictates to another. Agreement is something that is reached mutually. Agreement involves give and take and fair compromises.

An Agreement to Give 100 Percent

Agreement requires giving up "self." Marriage always requires heart doses of selfless giving.

Many people believe marriage is a fifty-fifty arrangement. Not so! Marriage is always a one hundred-one hundred arrangement; each person gives 100 percent.

Are You in Agreement?

Are you in agreement today with your spouse?

If you are contemplating marriage, are you in agreement on these six basics with your intended spouse?

The place to start in preventing and resolving conflict is to come to agreement on these basics.

In the next ten chapters, I am going to give you what I call "The Ten Commandments of Marriage." These are principles that work together to bring resolution to conflict. When put into place in marriage, they also can help prevent conflict.

As you read these principles, be aware that there is no sequence to these principles; one principle is not greater than the others. The ten work together "synergistically," which means that the sum of the effect of all ten working together is far greater than the ten working in isolation. Seek to implement *all* these principles into your marriage.

The good news is that each of these principles can be implemented starting today. You don't have to mature into any one of these commitments. Your marriage doesn't have to reach a new plateau before they begin to work.

Ask God to quicken these principles to your life. They are the building blocks that rest on the foundation laid in this chapter.

Seek agreement with your spouse about your need to "agree to agree." Come to a mutual decision:

- We *will* build our marriage on God's Word.

- We *will* leave the past in the past.

- We *will* "work" on our marriage.

- We *will* each seek to make the changes we know we personally need to make.

- When necessary, we *will* agree to disagree.

- We *will* each strive to give 100 percent to our marriage.

If you will make these basic commitments to each other, your foundation for marriage will be solid!

4

Revisit Your Commitment

Marriage Commandment #1:
Thou Shalt Keep Thy Wedding Vows

⊹‡⊱

*It is a snare for a man to devote rashly something as holy, and
afterward to reconsider his vows.*
—Proverbs 20:25

Too many people today are "reconsidering" their marriage vows; they are choosing to revise or alter them after the fact. Rather than reconsider what you have vowed to do, recommit yourself to doing what you said you would do!

A vow is a commitment, and a commitment is an agreement; it is a pledge to do something in the future. It is a willingness to *act* on a charge or trust.

The marriage vows that you made at the altar are a statement of your commitment to each other. Your vows, as the framework for your commitment, are an agreement about what is expected from each of you—not only what is expected by God and by each of you, but also what is expected by all those who witnessed your vows.

Many people who say "I do" can't really tell you later what they "did." You said that you would be committed, from that hour on, to do what you said you would do.

Some people seem to have selective amnesia—they remember only what they want to remember! If you were married in a Christian ceremony, you likely recited vows that went something like this:

> "Do you take this woman to be your wedded wife? Do you earnestly promise before God and these witnesses that you will love her, comfort her, honor her, and keep her, in sickness and health, and forsaking all others for her alone, you will perform to her all the respect that a husband owes to his wife, until God, by death, shall separate you?"

> "Do you take this man to be your wedded husband, and do you earnestly promise before God and these witnesses that you will love him, comfort him, honor him, obey him, in sickness and health, and forsaking all others for him alone, you will perform to him all the duties that a wife owes to her husband, until God, by death, shall separate you?"

The answer that a groom and bride make in response to these questions is generally, "I do." *I do* is a statement of com-

I do is a statement of commitment.

mitment. It's not only a statement made in that moment, but it's also a statement that is made as a foundational statement from that moment on. Every moment of the marriage from that first moment until separation by death is a moment in which "I do" applies.

Then, as part of actually making a wedding vow, with rings "in hand" that become rings "on hand," a couple generally recites words such as these:

> "I take thee to be my wedded wife, to have and to hold from this day forward, for better or worse, for richer or poorer, in sickness and health, to love and to cherish, until death do us part, according to God's holy ordinance, thereto I pledge thee my faith."

> "I take thee to be my wedded husband, to have and to hold from this day forward, for better or worse, for richer or

poorer, in sickness and health, to love and to cherish, until death do us part, according to God's holy ordinance, thereto I pledge thee my faith."

It's amazing how quickly we forget these two statements of commitment the minute trouble comes to the marriage.

Regardless of what the devil does or does not do, your commitment is based upon what *you* do.

Regardless of what people around you say or do, or don't say and don't do, your commitment is based upon what *you* do.

Regardless of what your spouse does, your commitment is based upon what *you* do.

Maybe your spouse didn't talk to you the way you wanted to be talked to.

Maybe your spouse didn't keep all the vows just the way you expected your spouse to keep them—just short of infidelity.

Maybe you didn't get the respect you wanted.

Maybe things didn't work out the way you anticipated.

Maybe your spouse didn't uphold his or her end of the vows.

The fact is, your commitment is based upon what *you* do.

You made a commitment.

You made a vow.

You said, "I do."

And *you* are where commitment begins and ends.

A Call to HOLY Matrimony

We call a marriage ceremony "holy matrimony." Holy matrimony is not possible for unholy people. The emphasis needs to be on "holy." Holy means "separate"; it refers to people being committed to God and separated by God's forgiveness from the sin of the world.

A lot of other adjectives drive people to a wedding ceremony. Some enter "emotional matrimony." Some enter "lustful matrimony."

Whatever it is that leads a couple to matrimony, that becomes the foundation of their matrimony.

Even if you did not truly enter "holy matrimony," as a Christian you are called to holy matrimony. You are called by God to live a marriage that is "different" from the model the world displays. You are called by God to live in a way that reflects God Himself.

The Implied Spiritual Commitment

Regardless of the exact wording of vows you actually recited to each other, if you were married in a Christian ceremony, you entered into a Christian marriage, and such a marriage has implicit vows based upon the New Testament Scriptures. The vows and pledge identified above are based upon the teachings of God's Word. In making vows to your spouse, you were making vows rooted in godly principles. You entered into a mutuality of relationship that is governed by God's "commandments," *even if you didn't know that's what you were doing.*

"But I didn't know that's what I was committing to," you may say.

My response is twofold. First, you *should* have known. Why were you making a vow before God and the witnesses to your marriage without knowing what it was that you were committing your life to do? The responsibility is yours for *knowing* the basics of your commitment; you are the one making the vow; you are the one reciting a pledge to your spouse; you are the one standing before God and witnesses to say "this is what I agree to do."

Second, it doesn't matter if you didn't know the details of all that was involved in your commitment. The principles of commitment that are at the heart of a marriage are still there, still true, and still in effect regardless of how well you know them, understand them, or can explain them. I don't know how gravity works. My ignorance of the law of gravity doesn't matter one iota if I step off a cliff. Gravity kicks in and works whether I understand it or not. The same is true for the principles of commitment for marriage. The implied commitment to God's principles is there whether you understand those principles fully, partly, or not at all.

Satan is intent, first and foremost when it comes to your marriage, on getting you to disavow your marriage vow. He strikes first at your *commitment.* If you are not committed, you cannot successfully resolve conflicts that arise in your marriage. Commitment is the beginning point; it is the most important point; it is the most potent factor in making your marriage strong and keeping it strong.

If you are not committed, you cannot successfully resolve conflicts that arise in your marriage.

Ask a husband or wife on the day of the wedding, "Do you really mean what you are about to say?" and 99 percent of them will say, "Yes."

Ask a husband or wife on the day of the wedding, "Are you confused about what you are committing your lives to do? Are you aware of the agreement into which you are entering with your words this day?" Ninety-nine percent of them will say, "I'm not confused. I know what I'm doing."

Ask a husband or wife on the day of the wedding, "Do you believe you can and will *do* what you are vowing to do today?" Ninety-nine percent of them will say, "Yes." Now, they may not be sure to that same degree that their spouse will uphold the other half of the vows, but they are generally convinced that they can uphold their part of the agreement.

But, along comes the day of conflict, and suddenly the very people who were so sure of their commitment on the day of their wedding begin to act confused and crazy, wavering in their commitment and unsure of their ability to keep their commitment.

Have you forgotten your commitment? Have you forgotten what you vowed to do?

Ask yourself today, "How have I been keeping my commitment to my spouse? Have I been doing my best to keep my commitment?"

In Jewish marriages, the marriage contract is a formal, written document presented at the time of the marriage. Many of these documents are beautifully illustrated and become family heirlooms through the centuries. A marriage contract is frequently hung on the wall of the new home that the couple establishes. This document of commitment is kept in plain sight for the couple to see day by day, for their children to see, and for all who enter their house to see.

Perhaps we Christians need to take a lesson from this long-standing Jewish custom. Can you even remember what it is that you agreed to do on your wedding day? Can you still recite the vows you made? Maybe you need to write out those vows and put them someplace where they are a ready reminder of what it is you agreed to do.

Revisit Your Commitment with Your Spouse

Revisit the commitment you made. Do it by yourself, and then revisit the commitment you made with your spouse. Revisit together the vows that you recited to each other.

God's Word records these words of the Lord to His people:

I will betroth you to Me forever; yes, I will betroth you to Me in righteousness and justice, in lovingkindness and mercy; I will betroth you to Me in faithfulness, and you shall know the LORD. (Hosea 2:19–20)

Is this your attitude as you go into marriage? Is this your attitude toward your spouse?

Are you committed to your marriage to lasting "forever"—all your lives, until death parts you?

Do you desire to live in righteousness and justice in your marriage? In other words, do you desire to do the "right thing" according to God's Word?

Do you desire to treat each other with loving-kindness and mercy?

Are you committed to being faithful to each other?

Are you committed to seeing God's image manifested in your marriage?

5

Face the Present Reality

Marriage Commandment #2:
Thou Shalt Discern the Deeper Reality

❖❖❖

*The thief does not come except to steal, and to kill, and to
destroy. I have come that they may have life, and that they may
have it more abundantly.*
— John 10:10

It's time to get real. Too many people have expectations for marriage that are totally unrealistic. One of these expectations is that all conflict can be avoided.

Face up to the fact that conflict in marriage is inevitable. For that matter, conflict is inevitable between any two people involved in a mutual task or who find themselves in a long-standing relationship.

Why?

Because the two people involved in a marriage are two *different* people. They have different likes and dislikes, different preferences and opinions about the way things should be done, different attitudes, different backgrounds, different personalities, different thought patterns, and different talents and abilities.

One of the major reasons cited in our judicial system for divorce is "irreconcilable differences." Differences are at the root of conflict.

Irreconcilable, however, is *not* a word that God authorizes for marriage. God's Word stands on the side of reconciliation; harmony; coming together; unity in spirit, purpose, and direction; a oneness of faith; a finding of common ground in Christ Jesus. God's commandments are for the purpose of helping people bridge their differences; His commandments bring people to a common ground in which they can live in mutual agreement for the betterment of all. God's law is not intended to restrict freedom as much as it is intended to create a safe, secure set of boundaries in which people can move freely to express their different gifts, talents, ideas, skills, and personalities.

If differences are emphasized, division occurs. A focus on differences spawns distrust, suspicion, frustration, anger, bitterness, and hatred.

If reconciliation and common ground are emphasized, wholeness occurs. A focus on reconciliation and common ground spawns trust, agreement, peace, harmony, a willingness to work together, understanding, compassion, and love.

A problem always arises if a person says, "My spouse and I just don't get along. It must not have been God's will for us to be together. Our marriage was a mistake."

Others conclude, "We're having conflict. This must be a sign that I picked the wrong person to marry."

People who draw these conclusions are people who see conflict as something no marriage should ever have. The fact is, *every* marriage has had conflict, does have conflict, and will have conflict. Conflict has nothing to do with whether you married the right person or the wrong person. It has to do with the fact that you are in a relationship with another person who has a mind, a mouth, a heart, and a will.

Every marriage has had conflict, does have conflict, and will have conflict.

My wife, Pamela, is one of the sweetest individuals I know, and I love her with all my heart. But let me assure you, my wife is capable of getting on my nerves. And guess what…as wonderful and as loving as I know I am, I know I'm capable of getting on her nerves! It doesn't matter how much you love your spouse or how much your spouse loves you; from time to time you are going to irritate each other, frustrate each other, argue with each other, have differences of opinion, or disappoint each other.

Any time a young couple comes to us for marital counseling and we hear them say, "Oh, we never fight. We get along so well. We agree about everything," Pamela and I look at each other with a little look that says, "Oh, you *will* argue. You *will* find that you don't agree about *everything*. You will have times when you aren't getting along so well." Conflict is part of the fabric of marriage for no other reason than two people are bound together by a vow before God, and there's a learning, maturing, developing, breaking, building, and growing process required for two people truly to become "one flesh," moving in the same direction with the same sense of purpose, calling, and focus.

Wake up and smell the coffee: you *are* going to have conflict, no matter how wonderful your relationship may be, how strong your love may be, how deeply you are committed to being married, or how intensely you desire to live in a state of marital bliss.

Discerning the Root of Conflict

Too many people, when they find themselves in conflict, allow the conflict to loom so large in their lives that they can't see the forest for the trees. If they step back a little from the conflict, they may gain some perspective on how they got to that tree in the forest. They may be able to look back in their lives and see mistakes that they made, mistakes that were made by their parents, or mistakes that were acquired from bad teaching, and so forth. But the real benefit in stepping back from the conflict a little is to see where the conflict is heading if it isn't resolved. As you step back from the conflict, you will see that the tree that looms so large in your life is about six inches from the edge of a sheer cliff!

Resolving Conflict in Marriage

If you want to know the real *root* of conflict, you have to take a look at the *result* of unresolved conflict. What is it that will ultimately happen to you if you don't resolve the conflict between you?

First, unresolved conflict doesn't evaporate into thin air. It goes underground into the deep parts of your soul. It festers, brews, grows, and becomes darker, sicker, meaner, and viler over time. It ferments and becomes a seething mixture of anger, frustration, bitterness, hatred, and deep disillusionment and disappointment. It can turn into depression, withdrawal, and sickness.

> Unresolved conflict doesn't evaporate into thin air.

Second, the more conflict that builds within you and between you as a couple, the more areas of your life will become sucked into that black hole of swirling conflict.

Third, the more you harbor conflict, the more your spouse will be diminished in "worth" in your eyes. You will lose respect for your spouse. You will care less, cherish your spouse less, and value your marriage less. Your will feel less affection and less love.

Fourth, you *will* eventually manifest your built-up anger, frustration, bitterness, disillusionment, or hatred. You will say things that you wish you could take back—or even worse, things that become just a "start" of all that you don't want to hold inside any longer. You will express your anger. You will build a wall of rejection. You will seek to inflict pain and heartache.

Fifth, your marriage will begin to crumble, and eventually it will collapse.

Most of us can close our eyes and see in our minds the images of those terrorist-hijacked planes slamming into the two towers of the World Trade Center on September 11, 2001. An engineer who helped construct those buildings was interviewed about the collapse of the buildings. He said, in effect, "People keep asking why the towers fell. To us as engineers, the question was, 'Why did the towers stay up as long as they did?'"

When those planes hit those towers, they hit with such force and so much flammable fuel that the fires they caused melted the steel in the framework. As the steel bowed outward, the weight of the concrete and steel on the floors above the fire fell down onto the floors below and caused them to collapse.

The same thing happens in marriage. When the fires of conflict build to the point of repeated explosions—when the flames of anger become so intense that they snuff out the oxygen of love and commitment—the vows that the couple made before God become weakened and bow outward. The weight of life's troubles, which every couple experiences, causes the commitment to collapse. Within a very short period of time, that marriage can turn into rubble.

Now, if that is the process of a *failure* to resolve conflict, we need to ask ourselves two main questions.

First, who desires your marriage to end up in a pile of dust and twisted emotional rubble? Who wants to bring ruin to your marriage?

In some cases, you might be quick to point to a person—perhaps a parent who was never in favor of the marriage or perhaps a person who is after your spouse and is seeking to break the two of you apart. But, even in those cases, you need to ask, who is *really* trying to tear apart what God has joined together?

The ultimate source of your conflict—the one who seeks to destroy your marriage—is the same one who wants to tear apart anything and everything that God has done, is doing, and ever will do. It's the devil himself.

The enemy of your soul is the enemy of your marriage.

What the devil desires to do in you—to tempt you away from Christ, to cause you to fall into sin, to have you collapse in your witness for Christ—he desires to do in your marriage. The devil who is out to steal from you, kill you, and destroy you as a person is the devil who is out to steal from your marriage, kill your marriage, and destroy any impact

> The enemy of your soul is the enemy of your marriage.

your successful, healthy marriage might have on this and the next generation. (See John 10:10.)

If you are experiencing ongoing conflict in your marriage, you need to go to God and do some spiritual warfare on behalf of yourself and your spouse. You need to get with another believer, or even with a small group of believers—people who will keep your prayers in confidence and who will pray with strong faith—and pray against the devil who is attacking your lives. You need to engage in some steady intercession that is marked by fasting and ongoing intense prayer.

If your spouse joins you in recognizing that the enemy of your souls is out to destroy your life together...great! Do battle together. Claim God's victory over this assault against you. Stand against the devil. The Bible says that if you will resist him, he will flee from you; and if you resist him together in your marriage, you are a powerful team of agreement. According to God's Word, he *must* depart from you. (See James 4:7 and Matthew 18:19.)

But, even if your spouse is blinded to the devil's work against you and your marriage, you must pray and intercede. Pray that your spouse's eyes will be opened to see the ultimate end of conflict and who is behind the conflict. Pray that your spouse will be set free from the clutches of the enemy who has him or her in bondage and who has established a stronghold against your marriage.

Facing the Lies of the Enemy

Every gardener knows that if you don't pull up a weed by the root, the weed will grow back. Unless you get to the heart of the matter and recognize the spiritual forces at work, the conflict will rise up again. One of the foremost ways the devil lies to you—and the manifestation of his character trait as a liar—is to fill your mind with false expectations. You need to pull up those false expectations by their roots and toss them on the trash heap!

The "Happily Ever After" Syndrome

The "happily ever after" syndrome probably comes from the fairy tales we heard as children. We tend to think that once two people get married, they will live in peace and harmony and joy for the rest of their days. After all, "they love each other" and have been through a wedding ceremony in which they pledged to love, honor, and cherish each other for the rest of their lives.

We never hear that "happily ever after" occurs only as the result of working at the relationship. We never hear that "happily ever after" happens only if we learn how to live together in a spirit of reconciliation and harmony. "Happily ever after" becomes the state of a couple's marriage only if both spouses lay down their pride and become selfless givers, pouring 100 percent of themselves into maintaining and strengthening their relationship. "Happily ever after" is never an automatic outcome of two lives joined together by a wedding ceremony. It is a state of being that comes far down the road as two people learn to resolve the conflicts that *will* rise between them. "Happily ever after" is a goal, not an automatic given.

The Perfect Person Syndrome

Many people go into a marriage relationship assuming that the marriage will be perfect because they concluded that they each are perfect people. The husband has concluded about himself, "I'm a perfect man." He has decided that his intended bride is a "perfect woman." How could the marriage be anything other than perfect? The woman does the same thing. She sees herself as being together and competent and "ready" to be married. She sees her Prince Charming as being the "perfect guy"—and if not perfect yet, then capable of becoming perfect under her guidance. At the very least, she concludes, "He's the perfect guy for me." So she assumes that since they are both perfect for each other, the marriage will be perfect.

Wrong! The husband is not perfect even if he thinks he is. The wife is not perfect even if she thinks she is. Both the husband and wife wake up one morning and face the reality: I did not marry a perfect person. And, shortly thereafter, both begin to wonder, "How did I ever think this was going to be a perfect marriage?"

Start with the fact that you aren't perfect. Not only that, but neither of you has ever been perfect or will ever be perfect this side of heaven. You may be better today than you once were—and that is certainly true if you are a Christian. You're better "saved" than you ever were "unsaved," but not because of anything you have done; rather, it is as a result of the work of Christ Jesus in you. If you continue to follow the Lord and seek to obey His Word, you will be better in the future than you are today. God is in the process of conforming you into the character likeness of Jesus Christ. (See Romans 8:28–29.) But right now, you are not a perfect person. Neither is your spouse. Therefore, your marriage is not going to be perfect.

Make it your goal to have a "good-and-getting-better" marriage. Make it your personal goal to be a "good-and-getting-better" husband or wife. Make it your personal goal to follow Christ more closely and to study and learn and apply His Word more directly to your everyday life.

There's simply no such thing as "perfection" or total wholeness; but God commands us to pursue His ideals and His wholeness with all our hearts, minds, and souls.

The "I Have a Right to Be Happy" Syndrome

Very closely related to the "happily ever after" syndrome is the "I have a right to be happy" syndrome. Tell me, where does Scripture say that you have a *right* to be happy? The Bible says you have a right to approach God boldly with your requests if you have received God's Son, Jesus Christ, as your Savior, and to make your petitions known. There's no provision in God's Word for *demanding* happiness. There's no promise of earthly happiness. There's promise of eternal life, and an abundant life on this earth that includes all the provision, protection, and empowerment that a person needs to successfully fulfill his or her role in God's kingdom. There's a promise that God will be with you always, through every kind of trial, trouble, and tribulation. There's a promise that you can overcome trouble by the blood of the Lamb and the power of His Word. But there's no promise that you will be "happy" at all times, in all circumstances, and with all people.

Even the Declaration of Independence says that a person has the right to *pursue* happiness. The right to pursue happiness is far different from a right to be happy.

What we do have is not a right to be happy, but a right to pursue the goodness of God and to choose to obey God's commandments and live according to God's statutes. Those who do so are in a position to be blessed by God and to enjoy the full favor and joy of His presence and of His working on their behalf.

How does this relate to your marriage?

You don't have a "right" to be happy in any relationship. What you have is a responsibility to do all you can to make the other person in the relationship happy.

My wife, Pamela, once said at a conference, "I don't have to be concerned about my happiness. I'm concerned about my husband's happiness. And when I make my husband's happiness my main concern, I'm happy. Why? Because he is making *my* happiness his concern, and he is doing all he can to make me happy. We make each other happy."

Any happiness that you experience in marriage will be as a result of two things:

• You are obeying what God has said to do as a spouse.

• You are in a relationship that is marked by reciprocity. Each of you is giving to the other the very thing you desire to receive back. It is in the reciprocity of giving and loving that we experience happiness.

Discernment Goes beyond Recognition

Recognition and discernment are two different things. Recognition is a process of the senses and the mind. It's a matter of perception and awareness. Recognition tells you what is happening. Discernment, in contrast, is a process of the spirit. It's a matter of spiritual understanding. Discernment tells you not only what is happening, but also why.

Most people who have conflict in their marriage recognize that they are having conflict. They know the air is so thick between them that you could cut that air with a knife. They know that they are tending to tear at each other like vultures and that they are causing high blood pressure in each other. They recognize, "We have a problem."

Very few people, including Christians, discern the real root and nature of the problem. They don't go to God with the petition, "Show me, God, why this is happening. Show me why I am responding and feeling the way I am responding and feeling. Show me why we are in conflict."

Discernment also has another dimension: spiritual discernment provides a solution to the problem. Discernment points a person away from the problem and to the answer. It applies wisdom to the problem.

When you have a problem in your marriage, go to God with it. Don't run to this person and that person, spreading your marital problems across the city. That doesn't do your spouse one bit of good. In fact, if your spouse discovers that this is what you have done, you are going to have even more problems in your marriage!

> **Discernment points a person away from the problem and to the answer.**

When you go to God with the problem, ask God to clarify any aspect of the problem you aren't understanding and need to understand. Ask Him to help you see clearly the root of the problem. Don't just tell God how you are feeling and what you think the problem is. Ask Him to show you how He sees the problem.

Then, ask God what to do about the problem. Ask Him to reveal to you how you are to pray about the problem, the solution you are to request, the intercession you need to do as you engage in spiritual warfare, and the commitment you need to make to ongoing prayer.

Don't Delay

Get to the root quickly. Recognize the devil at work. Deal with the little conflict before it becomes a big conflict. Don't allow the issue to carry on and grow.

Any unresolved conflict has the potential to grow. In fact, I can guarantee you that it will grow. Once you get the idea that something is wrong with the way your spouse is treating you, that idea will take on a life of its own because it's fueled by your life and your mind.

"He didn't show any affection to me" becomes "he doesn't care about me," which becomes "he doesn't love me," which becomes "he has never loved me."

"She didn't treat me with respect" becomes "she usually doesn't treat me with respect," which becomes "she never treats me with respect," which becomes "she has never respected me," which becomes "she doesn't know how to respect any man."

Anything that comes to your mind as a conflict, any conflict that continues to rise up in your heart, any conflict that creates in you a tension that doesn't find release in a few minutes is a conflict that needs to be addressed and addressed quickly.

A little sprout can become a big tree. Don't let it happen. Get that sprout uprooted while it has a tender, small, easily pulled-up root! If you don't, you're going to need a big shovel. You're going to need to go to all kinds of counselors to unravel the problem that has become so tangled you can't even tell where it started, and you surely can't tell where it's going to manifest itself next.

Once you have discerned the root of conflict, take on that root!

6

Be Faithful

Marriage Commandment #3:
Thou Shalt Be Faithful to Thy Spouse

❖❖❖

Watch, stand fast in the faith, be brave, be strong. Let all that
you do be done with love.
—1 Corinthians 16:13–14

When a person says, "Be faithful," the question arises almost immediately, "Faithful to what?"

First and foremost, you each need to choose to be faithful to God. Any time your faithfulness to God begins to slip, you are likely to find that your faithfulness to your spouse falters.

I'm not going to say it's impossible, but I do believe it is highly improbable that a nonbeliever can remain faithful to a spouse in marriage all his or her life. He may not commit adultery sexually, but he will find his affections wandering. He will find his conversations becoming flirtatious from time to time, his mind lustful, his desires fixed on impressing or winning the attention of first one person and then the next. The unbeliever simply has no *root of faithfulness* in his life, and therefore the *fruit of faithfulness* is not going to be manifested in his life.

Second, you need to be faithful to your spouse.

Just as faithfulness is a pillar for the believer's life, so faithfulness needs to be a pillar in a married person's life. Faithfulness builds and sustains the life of a relationship; it holds up the relationship. Faithfulness is the thread of life that continues to believe for the healing and reconciliation of a relationship that has gone through a difficult time. Because faithfulness is so important to a relationship, it is the one area of our lives where we hurt the most when it is no longer in place.

When a spouse betrays us and becomes unfaithful to us, we hurt in a way that is beyond all other hurt.

When a friend or a fellow Christian betrays us, we hurt in the midst of our anger and disappointment.

The only biblical reason given by Jesus for the dissolution of a marriage is unfaithfulness—a lack of fidelity, the committing of adultery, a total breach of trust. The reason is that faithfulness is at the core of marriage. If faithfulness is not intact, no other aspect of the marriage is going to function as intended by God.

How can you be committed to someone who is repeatedly unfaithful to you? How can you communicate at deep levels if you know that the person to whom you are communicating is likely to breach your confidence and be disloyal to you?

God's Help for Faithfulness

Why is faithfulness to God so important? Because when we choose with our wills to be faithful to God, He imparts to us the ability to be faithful. The willpower to be faithful no longer rests solely in the person; now the will of God Himself is involved. By the power of His Holy Spirit given to us, He helps us to remain faithful—not only in our walk before Him, but also in our walk with our spouse.

If you factor God out of your life, you factor out God's abiding presence with you, and you factor out His prevailing help. You cut yourself off from God's faithfulness to you as well as from His enduring power to help you endure in your faithfulness.

The Bible tells us,

No temptation has overtaken you except such as is common to man; but God is faithful, who will not allow you to be tempted beyond what you are able, but with the temptation will also make the way of escape, that you may be able to bear it. (1 Corinthians 10:13)

Now may the God of peace Himself sanctify you completely; and may your whole spirit, soul, and body be preserved blameless at the coming of our Lord Jesus Christ. He who calls you is faithful, who also will do it.
(1 Thessalonians 5:23–24)

But the Lord is faithful, who will establish you and guard you from the evil one. (2 Thessalonians 3:3)

Let us hold fast the confession of our hope without wavering, for He who promised is faithful. (Hebrews 10:23)

To Be Faithful Means to Be Steadfast

Steadfast is another word for faithful; it means "to be constant, dedicated, dependable, fast, stable, unswerving."

Steadfast in Loyalty

To be faithful means to be loyal. It means to stand by a person—no matter what. "No matter what" includes no matter what circumstances, no matter what behavior, no matter what you feel in your emotions that rise and fall, no matter what others say, no matter what temptations you encounter—no matter what.

> To be faithful means to be loyal.

To be faithful means to be devoted, true, and unwavering.

Loyalty is very often manifested in what you say about your spouse to others. Don't get into the blame game. Don't voice criticism of your spouse to other people. Take it to God. If you can't hear God on the matter, see a counselor who will keep what you say in the utmost confidence and who will give you godly counsel.

Anyone who runs down his or her spouse with constant public criticism and demeaning statements is disloyal. That person is being unfaithful to his or her spouse in words, even if not in deeds.

Loyalty is also manifested in your presence. Don't walk away in anger or frustration and think that, by your absence, you will manipulate your spouse into giving you what you want. You are being disloyal.

I once heard about a young woman who got married when she was seventeen, and during the first five years of her marriage, she threatened her husband with divorce more than a hundred times. That was by her admission; I suspect that if I had talked to her husband, it would have been even more times! Not only that, but she "moved back to mama" three times, staying at her parents' house from three days to two weeks at a time.

I asked, "Why did she do this?"

The answer was this: "She wasn't getting what she wanted from her husband—new clothes, a new place to live, new furniture—and this was the only way she thought she could coerce him into giving her what she wanted."

In the end, she got something she did not want, and that was her husband leaving her. He didn't threaten it; he just left and never came back.

What this young woman didn't realize was that every time she threatened her husband with divorce—either in her words or by her actions—she was sending a message to him: "You can't count on me. You can't count on me to be there for you, to remain with you, or to be steadfast in my loyalty to you." She was sending him a loud message of disloyalty and unfaithfulness.

Her lack of loyalty to her husband and her marriage caused her to be unfaithful—just as unfaithful as if she had entertained a sexual affair with another man.

If your spouse cannot count on you to be loyal in your words and in your deeds, what can your spouse count on?

Steadfast in Keeping Your Promises

To be faithful means that you willfully choose to keep the promises you made to your spouse before you married, the vows you spoke at the time of your wedding, and any subsequent promises you have made to your spouse.

Keeping your promises means keeping them consistently. What happens to trust if you promise to keep the house clean and you follow through and keep the house clean for two years, then one day wake up and decide that you no longer need to have a clean house? Your spouse is likely to say, "What else has my spouse decided she is no longer going to do? What else is it that she has promised to do—and may even be doing—that she won't be doing tomorrow?"

Now, this doesn't mean that you can't change some things as you go; but you need to discuss them, come to an agreement about them, and then do what it is that you have agreed together to do.

Steadfastness in Affection

Faithfulness also means that you are steadfast in your affection. Those who are steadfast are those who continue—strong, firm, unchanging—in maintaining the affection level of their marriage. If you have a medical situation that causes you to be unable to engage in sexual relations, that's one thing. Most medical situations are subject to healing, and when healing comes, sexual relations need to follow.

The excuses I have heard in marital counseling are rarely linked to a medical condition. Rather, they are couched in terms such as these: "He just doesn't turn me on anymore," "I'm tired," "I'm bored," "I don't enjoy sex anymore," "Kissing and hugging are just a waste of time—I want to get to the main course as quickly as possible."

Affection requires patience. If you skip romance, you will rarely have a satisfying, intimate relationship.

Affection requires persistence. If you aren't in the mood today, figure out why, and change the conditions of your life so you will be in the mood tomorrow.

Affection requires creativity. If what you've done in the past to turn each other on is no longer working, try something new!

A spouse never has the right to say several months or years into a relationship, "I'm tired of showing affection. I'm finished with hugging and kissing and sexual intercourse." A spouse never has the right to say, "I don't want to make love to you anymore." Showing affection is never a "been there, done that" matter!

If you need some advice on how to satisfy your spouse, if you need medication to help you perform sexually, if you need counseling on how to satisfy your spouse in this area of your married life, get the help you need.

Faithfulness Is a Choice

Only you can choose to be faithful. Nobody else can make you or force you to be faithful. Faithfulness begins in *your* heart and mind, and it is then manifested in your outward actions.

The sooner you come to the conclusion that you are going to be faithful to God and to your spouse, the sooner you are going to resolve conflict when it arises...and the stronger your marriage is going to be. As long as there is any doubt about whether you are choosing to be faithful, there will always be a cloud of question over your marriage. There also will be a crack in the wall, a corner missing from the hedge of protection God seeks to establish around your marriage. There will always be a tiny crack in the door through which temptation can come blasting in.

The choice is not one you make only once. It is an ongoing choice because faithfulness is ongoing.

You never reach the point where you say, "Well, I've been fully faithful. I can stop being faithful now." By the very definition of the word, faithfulness is something you do until the day you die. Or, as you said in your marriage vows, until the day when you are separated by death. Your faithfulness to the Lord has only one expiration date—your death date. You are called to be faithful to the Lord every day of your life until the moment you enter into

Your faithfulness to the Lord has only one expiration date— your death date.

eternity. In like manner, you are called to be faithful to your spouse until the day you die or your spouse dies, whichever comes first. Your release from faithfulness to your marriage vows comes only at death.

7

Talk about It

Marriage Commandment #4:
Thou Shalt Communicate

❖❖❖

Be of the same mind in the Lord.
—Philippians 4:2

One time in a counseling session, I asked a woman if she knew when her marriage troubles had entered the serious stage. She said, "I know the precise moment."

"When was it?" I asked.

She said, "It was the day we both just sighed and walked away and decided the problem wasn't worth talking about anymore."

Communication is vital to a marriage. It is the means to preventing most conflicts, and it is the means to keeping most conflicts from escalating. It is the way two people build understanding and become of "one mind" regarding the basic agreements that are at the very heart of their relationship.

Let me give you a very basic definition of communication: communication is a process by which information is exchanged between individuals through a common system of symbols, signs, speech, and behavior. You communicate by what you say and by how you act, how you respond, how you *behave*.

> You communicate by what you say and by how you act.

One of the most potent forms of communication is verbal communication. It is potent because it is the form of communication that has the potential for bringing about the greatest clarity of understanding. Gestures—from raised eyebrows to shrugs of the shoulder—are subject to a great deal of misinterpretation. Walking out of the room in the heat of an argument, throwing up your hands, grunting, crying, growling, staring at the ceiling—all these are "signs" that communicate, but exactly *what* is communicated is often unclear. Staying away from home for several days, coming in at two o'clock in the morning, wearing a shirt that has lipstick on the collar, dropping an unexplained key as you open your purse or empty your pocket—all these behaviors communicate, but not with clarity. There's a great deal of room for interpretation and misinterpretation.

Can You Talk to Your Spouse?

Can you talk to your spouse? If not, you and your spouse are missing out on the greatest tool for building a good marriage.

The fact is, every person I've ever counseled about marriage can communicate if he or she really wants something. The person who says he has trouble communicating with a spouse has absolutely no trouble communicating what he wants to say to a waitress when ordering from a menu in a restaurant, what he wants to say to the dry cleaner who ruins his suit, what he wants to say to the person who is sitting in his reserved seat at the ball game, or what he wants to say to the clerk who gives back the wrong change.

It's not that you don't know how to communicate. Don't tell me, "I just don't know how to talk to him," or "I just don't know what to say to her." Yes, you do. You knew enough about how to talk to him or what to say to her to get to the altar to recite your marriage vows!

It's not that you don't know how to communicate. Rather, you don't want to make the effort to communicate because your feelings are on the line, you are feeling vulnerable, or you believe that what you are likely to hear back isn't what you want to hear.

One of satan's great lies is that two people who are able to communicate all the way down the aisle to the marriage altar can suddenly become unable to communicate with each other as they walk back up the aisle away from the marriage altar and out the door of the church into the world outside.

Main Issues for Discussion

What are some of the things you need to learn to communicate about verbally? Five of the biggest issues requiring communication in a marriage tend to be the following: money, children, sex, faith, and extended family members.

Money

It's amazing to me that people who have absolutely no trouble talking about money on the job or in the marketplace—buying and selling, negotiating deals, bargaining on a price—suddenly have trouble talking about money with their spouse.

A man once said to me, "I am the manager of a department that has twenty people in it, and I have authority over a budget of nearly a half million dollars. I live in a world of production schedules and quotas and budgetary constraints. But when I try to talk to my wife about a budget, we end up going around in circles."

Why do we have difficulty talking to our spouses about money? Because there are feelings on the line. Some of those feelings are guilt (for overspending), anger (that your spouse overspent the budget), confusion (about how to spend and save and invest), and a lack of control or willpower when it comes to buying. Some of the feelings are ones associated with our self-esteem, or lack of it. Some of the feelings are frustration and disappointment, especially when it comes to the income side of the ledger. Some of the feelings are ones of despair or of being overwhelmed, especially if a crisis has sapped or zapped the family's finances.

Children

I've had teachers, court advocates, and police officers who work in juvenile detention tell me that they have no difficulty at all communicating to children or about children "on the job," but they admit that they never had a good conversation with their spouse about how they intended to raise the children they hoped to have.

One woman said to me, "Before we got married, we talked about how many children we wanted to have and about our hopes for having at least one boy and one girl. But we never talked about the *reasons* we wanted to have children or the ways we intended to discipline our children, educate our children, or lead our children to Christ." She was shocked later to discover that she and her husband were on two different wavelengths when it came to raising children.

Another woman said to me, "I already had two children when we got married. What's the point of talking about children? The children were already there; they were half raised. I just figured I'd continue to do what I had been doing, and he'd fall in line." She was greatly saddened to discover that her husband didn't "fall in line" as she had anticipated.

A man once said to me, "I didn't want kids, but I knew that she did. So I didn't say anything. I was afraid she wouldn't marry me if I said I didn't want any children. And I guess in the back of my mind I thought I might also change my mind down the line." He was greatly puzzled at the anger he felt when his wife got pregnant—as if that anger had nothing to do with what he had been feeling but hadn't communicated prior to their wedding.

Why don't engaged people and married people talk about children? Because there are feelings involved—feelings of potential rejection ("I'm not sure my spouse or future spouse will agree with me—he might reject me if I speak what I truly believe or what I truly want to do in this area"), ambivalence (from "I don't know if I want children" to "I don't know how I want to discipline my children"), or guilt ("I'm already pregnant, so it's too late now to talk about children").

Sex

Men will talk to other men about sex—sex they've had, sex they wish they could have, sex they are planning to have. Women also talk to other women about sexual issues—their concerns and language may be a little different from that of men, but they talk nonetheless. But do men and women talk about sex before marriage? Do they talk about sex after marriage? Not as much as you might think.

One woman in a marriage counseling session said to us, "I've been married for five years, and I've never told my husband what I do and don't like in bed."

A man once said to us, "I wish we had a lot more sex in our marriage." I said, "Have you told your wife that?" He said, "Heavens, no. If I told her that, she'd probably run from the house, and I'd never see her again." What he didn't know—and what we didn't tell him because of our commitment to confidentiality in counseling—was that his wife had been to see us ten days before and had voiced the very same desire: "I wish we had more sex in our marriage!" Trust me, I advised this man to bring his wife the next time he came for a counseling appointment. That was a problem that was easy to resolve!

Why don't married couples talk about sex? There are too many feelings—too many desires, needs, hopes, and concerns about rejection on the line. There's vulnerability and feelings of being "exposed" to the other person. It's amazing—people who will expose their physical bodies to each other very often won't expose their innermost feelings to each other. We're *afraid* to do so.

Faith

A fourth issue that is vital for communication is the area of faith. A woman once said to me, "He carried a Bible to church, so I assumed he was a Christian. But when I said something to him later about this, he said, 'Oh no, I never claimed to be a Christian. I have a Bible, and I went to church with you because that's what I knew *you* wanted. I never told you I was a Christian.'"

Why don't engaged and married couples talk about their faith? Very often, feelings are in the way. These feelings run deep—they are at the core of a person. They relate to how people feel about

God and how they believe God feels about them, and such emotions always include feelings about how they feel toward others and toward themselves. Feelings get in the way of giving voice to their greatest hopes, fears, concerns, dreams, failures, and beliefs.

Family Members

Invariably, a person marries into a family and discovers that at least one member of that family is "crazy." I don't mean crazy in the sense of being institutionalized in a psychiatric hospital, but crazy in other ways—offbeat, eccentric, strange. Or perhaps the craziness manifests in the way family members try to control your life and the life of your spouse, the way they demand attention or assistance at inopportune times or in inappropriate degrees, the way they express anger, or the way they seek to control your children (usually their grandchildren).

Before I really got to know my father-in-law, I thought he was crazy. We disagreed on a couple of things in the very early months of my marriage to his daughter, and I thought he was a violent, rigid, hard man—and I was scared to be around him. When I got to know him, though, I found that he was a deeply caring and kind man and that he had no intent whatsoever of doing harm to me. He just wanted to make sure I was taking good care of his daughter.

Every couple needs to communicate about how they will deal with family members. They need to discuss where the boundaries are going to be drawn. When we marry, we are to leave our parents and cleave to our spouses. (See Matthew 19:5.) Some people have a difficult time leaving mom or dad; they don't know how to quit being dependent on what their parents think or do. Some parents have a difficult time cutting the apron strings or purse strings. Some people continue to listen to their parents and to do what mom and dad dictate more than they communicate with their spouse and do what the two of them decide is right for their marriage and their family.

I love my parents with all my heart. I have no desire to rebel against them in any way. But I guarantee you this, if my parents had tried to interfere in my marriage, I would have chosen not to see them for a while. I would have put some distance between us.

I encounter people all the time who allow their parents to speak about their spouse as if that person has four legs and a tail. They allow their parents to speak ill about what their spouse does, says, or wears. They have nothing good to say about how their child's spouse cooks, keeps house, provides an income, spends his spare time, or chooses friends and associates.

I encounter people who go to special events with their parents and choose to spend time with their parents rather than spend time with their spouse. Sometimes they do this out of guilty feelings or pressure; sometimes they do this just to "get away" from their spouse.

I encounter people who run to their parents' house at the first instance of conflict rather than stay at home and communicate with their spouse about how to resolve their conflict.

Let me ask you, what do any of these approaches and behaviors have to do with "honoring" your spouse? The truth is, they have nothing to do with bringing honor to your spouse. The exact opposite is true—if you allow others to speak ill of your spouse, take you away from time with your spouse, or drive a wedge between you and your spouse, you are bringing dishonor to your spouse. You are allowing your spouse to be reduced in your mind and in the mind of any person who hears the negative talk or sees the dishonoring behavior; and, ultimately, you are reducing the integrity, reputation, and character of your spouse in your spouse's mind. You are saying, in effect, "You aren't worth my time. You aren't worth my commitment. You aren't worth my respect. You aren't worthy of any praise or appreciation or effort."

I've heard men say to their wives, "I love you, but my mama is my number-one girl." I've heard women say to their husbands, "I'm a daddy's girl, and I'll always be a daddy's girl." Let me assure you, neither of these statements is biblical! When you marry, sir, your wife becomes your number-one girl. When you marry, ma'am, you become your husband's girl.

"But," a man once argued with me in a marriage counseling session, "my daddy died when I was young. I've taken care of my mother all my life. Who's going to fix her house or take her places if I don't?"

I said to him, "She's a grown woman. She can find somebody else to fix her house and take her places. If you were dead, she'd figure it out. If you think you still need to take care of your mother as your top priority—jumping at her beck and call at any time of the day or night—then don't marry. When you marry, your wife becomes your number-one priority."

As a married couple, you need to communicate about how you will handle family reunions, holiday times (and where you are going to spend certain holidays), and the relationship between your parents and your children (how much "spoiling" or "disciplining" of your children you will allow from your parents). You need to communicate about the crazy brother who always shows up drunk asking for twenty dollars. You need to communicate about the crazy sister who seems to have one child after another out of wedlock, and who shows up on your doorstep begging you to take care of those children.

Again, feelings run deep when family members are involved. If you don't get things squared away with your spouse *before* you get married, it's going to be even harder to reach agreement about how to relate to your family members after you get married. Hurt feelings will multiply. Guilt is mixed in there. Anger is likely. Frustration is always the undercurrent.

Communicate, communicate, communicate. And once you have reached agreement with your spouse about how to deal with certain family members, communicate about a way to communicate your decision to the family members involved. Discuss when, and how, and to whom you should say what. Then, communicate your decision. Take a stand. Draw a boundary.

Strip Away Some of the Emotions

Repeatedly in the last few pages I've mentioned the reason these very important issues for communication are often ignored or downplayed in a marriage: emotions. These five vital areas for communication are areas in which emotions run deep. At times, we need to strip away some of the emotion from our communication in order to really be heard and to hear.

When our feelings get in the way of our communication, two things tend to happen. First, we tend to hold in our feelings and fail to communicate. We live in denial; we both deny having feelings, and we deny opportunities to talk. We say "no" when our spouse asks, "Is there something on your mind?" The truth is that the issue is very much on our mind, and, even more so, the issue is eating away at our heart.

> At times, we need to take the emotion out of our communication.

The more we hold our feelings in, the more they build up pressure in us, and the day will come when our feelings will explode. Emotions always find a "vent" somewhere, sometime, in some situation; and the greater the pressure that has built up over time, the greater the explosion of those emotions is likely to be.

The second thing that happens when feelings get in the way of our communication is that our communication becomes oversaturated with feeling. The deeper and more intense our feelings, and the greater the importance we place upon an issue, the less likely we are to be able to discuss an issue with cool, calm rationality. If intense feelings are involved, we tend to cry or shout or pout or whine when we communicate.

Certainly, we were made to have emotions and were intended by our Creator to express those emotions. We were not, however, made by our Creator to be ruled by our emotions. We are to be in control of our emotions and not let our emotions be in control of us. Many of the issues related to communication need to be stripped of some of their emotional heat so we can clearly see the issues that lie before us. Then we can share accurate information with each other in a way that is beneficial, productive, and healthful. What happens when there's too much heat rising from something? Usually there's steam or a vapor that creates a mirage. If there's too much steam, people get burned, and nobody sees clearly. If there's a mirage, goals and visions for a couple's life together get blurred, and nobody sees clearly.

For communication to be *clear,* for both parties in the communication to be helped more than hurt, and for communication to result in a positive forward motion for the relationship, some of the feelings associated with our communication need to be stripped away.

Tempers need to cool before communicating.

Tears need to be shed in advance of communicating.

Hurt feelings need to be bathed in prayer before communicating.

Fears need to be faced with faith before communicating.

But then, once the feelings have been stripped away, we need to muster our courage and choose to communicate.

We need to express what we believe and why.

We need to express our hopes and our dreams.

We need to express our concerns and our fears.

We need to tell what we have done and how we have felt, and we need to admit our own weaknesses even as we acknowledge our strengths.

If you feel fear or reluctance today in communicating something to your spouse, ask yourself, "Why can't I communicate in this area?" Face up to the feelings that are associated with the words you want to say but are reluctant to say.

Take those feelings to the Lord. Talk to Him about the way you are feeling. Ask Him to help you deal with your fears, your anticipation that you will be rejected, your low self-worth, your guilt. Ask Him to give you faith, courage, self-valuing love, and forgiveness.

Dealing Positively with Excess Emotions

Get rid of some of the emotion in a positive way. Go for a brisk walk. Cry into your pillow. Scream into your pillow. Pound your fist into a punching bag at the gym or take out your frustration by swimming an extra lap in the pool or running an extra mile.

Then, role play with God what you'd like to say to your spouse—rehearse the words, and as you do, listen to your own arguments and language. Analyze how *you* would respond if someone said to you what you'd like to say to another person.

If you don't know what you'd like to say, go to God's Word to see what it says on the issue. Talk to a Christian mentor or counselor to get wise advice. Settle in your own heart and mind what you believe, what you think, and what you'd like to see accomplished in a conversation on the topic that is troubling you.

Come up with an opening line. A man once said to me, "I know what I want to say at the end of our conversation. I just need an opening line." This man had absolutely no difficulty coming up with a reason to get this woman to go out with him the first time. I found it amazing that he didn't know how to bring up the subject he wanted to broach. I said, "If she was a total stranger whom you were being asked to counsel or advise, what would you say?" He thought for a moment, then he suddenly perked up and said, "Thanks. That's exactly what I'm going to say to her." I still don't know what he thought to say or if he said it, but the advice is good: how would *you* bring up the subject to a total stranger you were asked to counsel or give advice?

Decision-Making and Problem-Solving

Two of the main areas in which we need good communication are decision-making and problem-solving.

Don't know what to fix for dinner? Ask your spouse what he'd like to have. If he doesn't have an answer, tell your spouse what you are planning to fix and get a response. I know a newlywed who fixed a beautiful meal for her husband—she had it all ready when he got home from work. The table was set, the candles lit; everything was just right. He took one look at the main course and said, "I can't eat this."

She said, "What do you mean, you can't eat this?"

He said, "I'm allergic to this."

"Why didn't you tell me you were allergic to this?"

"You didn't ask me."

The result was she stormed into the kitchen feeling angry, hurt, rejected, and frustrated, and then angry at herself for feeling hurt, rejected, and frustrated. He sat at the kitchen table feeling sad, frustrated at his own allergy, and wondering what to do to make it right. Meanwhile, a perfectly good meal was going to waste.

Simple communication about a basic decision-making issue would have prevented that problem. Simply asking, "Tell me what you *can* eat and what you *like* to eat," would have resulted in a list that could have kept her busy in the kitchen for six months!

Is there an issue too petty? No.

Is there an issue too big? No.

Most of us know how we would solve a problem if we were single. Most of us know which decision we would make if we were single.

But we never stop to think that we aren't single anymore and that another person is involved in solving the problem and making the decision. We need to factor in that other person before we go off "doing our own thing."

Where do we begin?

Ask. Ask your spouse what he or she thinks. Ask your spouse what decision he'd make if he were alone in the decision-making process, and then ask what decision he thinks is right for the two of you. Ask your spouse how she would solve a problem if she were alone in the problem-solving process, and then ask what solution she thinks is right for the two of you.

Give your own "first solution" or "first response" opinions regarding decisions and problems that you face as a couple. Let your spouse know that this is how you are seeing things *at the present time*. Get your spouse's input before you reach a final decision. Be open to your spouse's suggestions, reasons, concerns, and expressed desires. The more you discuss a problem or decision with your spouse before taking action, the more likely you are to make a wise decision that benefits both of you, and the more likely you are to be committed as a couple to the decision you make.

Decisions take communication—in their formation, in their enactment, and in their "amendment" down the line. We need to communicate before we make a decision. We need to communicate about what we are going to do. And if our decision proves to be a wrong decision, or a less-than-best decision, we need to be open to changing our decision. Above all, we need to deal with decisions in a way that is mutually agreeable.

Solutions take communication—both in their discovery and in their implementation. We need to communicate about why we think a certain problem has arisen, what factors are involved in coming to a solution, and how to start a process of solving the problem, even if we can't come up with a definitive solution immediately. We need to approach solutions to problems in a way that says, "We're in this problem together. Let's figure out a way to get out of this problem together."

Goal Accomplishment Requires Communication

Very little communication is necessary for one person in a marriage to set a goal. For two people to set and pursue the same goal takes a great deal of communication!

Dreams and wishes take little time, energy, or money. The accomplishment of goals, however, requires a great deal of time, energy, skill, and, in many cases, money. The accomplishment of goals requires sacrifice. The time you spend pursuing your goal is time that will have to come from somewhere—and in all likelihood it will come from your personal time, not the time you spend at a job earning money to pay your basic bills. The energy you need to pursue a goal is going to come from somewhere; again, it's likely to come from the energy you might otherwise use for family activities. The money you need to get the education, training, skills, or experience necessary to reach a goal will come from somewhere—and it's likely going to be money that would otherwise be spent on some of life's luxuries, such as an extra business suit, a weekend trip, a piece of jewelry, or some other item that you'd like to have but can't have because the money is being poured into the pursuit of a dream. What an individual in a marriage sacrifices in the pursuit of a dream is nearly always what a couple or a family sacrifices in the pursuit of a dream.

If you have a lifelong goal, ambition, or dream, you must convey that to your spouse or intended spouse. Make sure your spouse is on the same page with you regarding the pursuit of your dream.

I recently heard about a couple who was facing severe financial problems as the result of a building contractor bailing out on them halfway through a major remodeling job. As you might suspect, they had already paid him for completion of the job. In the midst of their struggles to get their home repaired and back into a livable state, the husband announced to his wife that he was tired of his job and that he needed to return to school full-time to pursue another career, one that he said was a "lifelong dream." The wife said, "Are you kidding?" Actually, she said something much stronger than that—she was not at all in agreement with that goal.

Now, it wasn't that this wife didn't want her husband to succeed in the career of his dreams or go back to school. The timing was off. That particular year in their marriage was not the time to quit a job and take out loans to pay for tuition.

Don't limit your discussion of goals to *what* you want to do. Communicate also about *when* and *how* you intend to pursue your goals until they are accomplished.

Sooner Rather than Later

A man once shared with me that his wife had come to him and said, "I've been in disobedience to God. I need to do what God has called me to do."

"And what is it God has called her to do?" I asked.

He said, "Preach. She says she's called to be a preacher."

"As an evangelist? A pastor? A speaker for special events?"

"Just preach," he said. "She's talking about going to Bible school."

"What do you think about that?" I asked.

"Well, I wish she would have told me about this before we had three children. I wish she had told me about this before she spent ten years as my secretary and bookkeeper, helping me establish our landscaping business. I married a woman who told me she wanted to be a wife, mother, and businesswoman. I thought she was doing what she had said she wanted to do before we got married. Now she tells me that she said those things to me because she thought I wanted to hear those things, when all the time she really wanted to be a traveling evangelist."

"What have you said to her?" I asked.

"I asked her, 'What did you think was going to happen by your living out one thing and wishing for another?' And she said, 'Well, I was hoping you'd get a call from God to go into the ministry and we could be co-pastors.' I said, 'Did I ever tell you that God had called me into the ministry? Didn't I tell you that I felt God had placed it in my heart to have a landscaping business that was prosperous to the point where I could help fund ministry activities, as well as bring some beauty to church properties and retreat facilities? I've been living out my goals—the goals I shared with you before we got married.'"

Have a sense of purpose for your own life before you go into a marriage. Know what you want. Know what God has called you to do. Have a direction for your life. And as God reveals to you certain goals for your life, be open in sharing those goals *before* you get married.

Don't expect God to change your spouse after you marry so that you can pursue goals you want to accomplish. Don't expect God to conform another person to your will or desires. God is in the process of conforming each of us to *His* will and desires. He doesn't place a lifetime dream or goal in one person's heart and a completely contrary dream or goal in another person's heart, and then expect one person to give up his or her goal. No! He will bring two people together who can pursue a *shared* vision for their lives. He brings people together who have complementary skills, dreams, and talents, so that *together* they might pursue a dream that is in keeping with each of their individual dreams, and yet one that is ultimately bigger than either of their individual dreams.

You cannot achieve a goal all by yourself. It's just not possible. You can't accomplish anything of significance without assistance from others. It might be information or training they provide for you, financial help they give you, time they give to baby-sit your children so you can go to night school, food they bring to you so you can study for examinations, or encouragement they offer to you in times when you feel like giving up. Your spouse needs to be your number-one ally and helper in the pursuit of a goal that will be *mutually beneficial to both of you*. To receive and to sustain the help of a spouse in pursuit of a goal takes communication.

Communicating with Signs and Symbols

Some people say one thing, but their body language says something entirely different. Don't say "I love you" with your lips and then roll your eyes in a way that says "I detest you." Don't say "everything's fine" with your lips and then walk around the house moping and sighing and giving your spouse the silent treatment.

One of the things I hear repeatedly from couples is, "I need my space."

Trust me, that is *not* the signal that the person gave prior to getting married. Prior to getting married, most couples want to

Marriage is not about being alone. It's about being together.

be as close to each other as they can be—all the time! They practically sit on top of each other at the movie theater; they hold on to each other as if they might fall down without the other while they walk down the street; they sit so close to each other in the car that you can't tell if there's one or two people driving—they can't spend enough time with each other. But, after the wedding..."I need my space. Don't touch me. Leave me be. I need 'alone time.'"

Marriage is not about being alone. It's about being together.

Marriage is not about having individual space. It's about learning how to share space.

Marriage is not about having your own schedule. It's about living out a mutual schedule so that each of you takes into consideration the obligations, responsibilities, desires, and needs of the other person.

Marriage is not about being untouchable, remote, aloof, or mute. It's about living in intimacy together—talking, hugging, kissing, holding, and being together.

If you want a great deal of space that is entirely yours to control, if you want an open-ended schedule that is entirely yours to plan, if you want time that is entirely yours to use, then don't get married. Marriage is about sharing and communicating about how you will arrange your shared space, adjust your shared schedules, and spend your shared lifetime.

A Lifelong Process

Communication is a lifelong process. You never become so good at communicating that you can stop communicating! The moment you stop communicating is the moment when you are no longer good at communicating! A "failure" to communicate always creates a "problem" in communication.

> Communication is a lifelong process.

Repeated communication of the wrong message also can create a problem.

Rather than say consistently, "You never listen to me," say consistently, "I appreciate the times you listen to me."

Rather than say consistently, "You and I are always opposites," say consistently, "I'm so glad we have so many areas of agreement in our marriage."

Rather than say consistently, "You never treat me right," say consistently, "I feel very special when you treat me like a beloved creation of God."

What you speak to your marriage and to your spouse *consistently* is going to be what becomes manifested in your marriage.

As a part of your communication, it is absolutely necessary that you both tell the truth—the whole truth and nothing but the truth. That leads us to the next area important to resolving conflict....

8

Tell the Truth and Keep No Secrets

Marriage Commandment #5:
Thou Shalt Build Trust by Telling the Truth

You shall know the truth, and the truth shall make you free.
—John 8:32

Our military in the United States of America may have a policy of "don't ask, don't tell" on certain issues, but let me assure you, a policy of "don't ask, don't tell" in a marriage can be absolutely deadly to the relationship.

A huge part of being faithful means being trustworthy. And nobody can trust a person who doesn't tell the truth. In your marriage, it is absolutely vital that both spouses are willing to tell each other the truth.

I'm not referring to your telling your spouse what you believe to be the truth about somebody else's business, the truth underlying world issues, or even the truth about your spouse's behavior and the reasons for it. I'm referring to telling the truth about *yourself*—your ideas and feelings, your behavior, your plans, your activities, your whereabouts, and your relationships.

> A policy of "don't ask, don't tell" can be absolutely deadly to a marriage.

A husband must be willing to tell the truth about himself as a man and a husband. The wife must be willing to tell the truth about herself as a woman and a wife. Both persons must be willing to be vulnerable to the other. They must be willing to reveal what they dream about accomplishing, what they believe, what they hope for, what bothers them, what fears torment them, what nightmares haunt them.

A good marriage is also one in which both persons are willing to tell the truth about their comings and goings, about what they are doing, about who they are with. A good marriage is one in which both people are open and transparent with the other. They don't have secrets.

If you want to avoid a great deal of conflict in your marriage, don't hide things from your spouse.

Don't hide phone numbers from your spouse.

Don't hide purchases you've made that you know took you over your budget.

Don't hide "friends" from your spouse.

Don't hide your activities from your spouse.

Don't hide your whereabouts from your spouse.

"But, my spouse doesn't have any right to know where I am all the time," you may say.

The fact is, your spouse *does* have that right by virtue that he or she is your spouse. Your spouse is one flesh with you. Your spouse needs to know where you are, what you're doing, who you are hanging out with, what you are buying, and who you are in contact with. One of the most effective ways to introduce conflict into your relationship with your spouse is to keep secrets from your spouse.

> If you want to avoid a great deal of conflict in your marriage, dont hide things from your spouse.

The truth will eventually come to light. It may not be today or tomorrow, but the truth will emerge sooner or later. And when it does, you're going to find yourself scrambling for a flimsy excuse that will never hold up.

Now, I'm not talking about hiding a Christmas present from your spouse, keeping it a secret that your spouse's best friend is planning to come visit, or that you are planning a surprise birthday party for your spouse. I'm talking about hiding things from your spouse because you don't want to answer questions about your character or behavior that are related to that thing you are hiding.

I'm talking about hiding bad habits.

I'm talking about bad associations.

I'm talking about going places you know you shouldn't be going and doing things that you know before God you shouldn't be doing.

If you have something to hide, chances are you shouldn't be doing what you're hiding!

If you have something to hide, face the fact that you are living a lie. You are saying one thing and doing another. You are in serious danger of destroying the trust your spouse has in you.

This is especially true if you are hiding a relationship with a person of the opposite sex.

Truthfulness Builds Trust

A wife needs to be able to trust her husband's words. She must be able to know with complete assurance in her heart that her husband is faithful to her sexually, but there's so much more to fidelity and trustworthiness than remaining sexually faithful.

A wife needs to be able to have confidence in the truthfulness of her husband. When he says, "I'm going to pay the bills rather than gamble this money away or spend it on my personal desires," she has to trust that he will follow through and pay the bills!

A wife needs to be able to trust her husband when he says, "I'm going to play golf this Saturday morning." She needs to have confidence that if she really needs him, she can find him at the golf course and not down at the local bar or off at the fishing pond with his buddies.

A wife needs to be able to count on the truthfulness of her husband when he says, "I'll discuss that with you as soon as the game is off." When the game is over, he needs to be true to his word and discuss the issue with his wife. It's a matter of *trustworthiness*.

A wife needs to be able to trust her husband when he says, "You can come to me and tell me anything." She has to trust that he won't freak out or fly off the handle if she comes to him to say, "I have a problem," "I have some feelings that I don't know how to handle," or "I'm upset." In a very practical way, she needs to trust that her husband will remain calm and reasonable if she comes and says, "I bought this dress at the mall today." She needs to be able to trust her husband with an honest expression of her own emotions and concerns, without any put-down or dismissal statement such as "I can't handle this."

The same is true in reverse, of course. A husband needs to be able to trust that his wife is telling him the truth—the whole truth and nothing but the truth. He needs to be able to trust her with their money and possessions. He needs to be able to place full confidence in her ability to keep his secrets and be loyal to him as she talks to others.

For a person to "submit" to another person, trust must be in place. You can't submit to someone you don't trust. And you can't trust a person who is untrue to his or her words or who fails to have integrity when it comes to following through on that word.

Be True to Your Word

One of the most basic definitions of integrity is this: say what you mean, and do what you say. The person who follows through and does what he says he is going to do is a person you can trust.

Say what you mean, and do what you say. Keep your promises. Don't make a promise you don't intend to keep. And once that promise leaves your lips, keep it!

The Bible tells us that God gave us His "Word"—His spoken word in the Old Testament laws and commandments, His living word in the Son, Jesus Christ, and His ongoing, anointed word that speaks in our hearts by the revelation and power of the Holy Spirit. God gave us His Word and has been true and faithful to the Word He gave. God's Word represents God Himself.

We are called to do the same. Don't give your word unless you intend to be true and faithful to your word. Don't speak a word about your *intent* to do something unless you take steps to follow through on that intent and actually do the thing you said you were going to do. Your word represents you.

Your word represents you.

When we began building our second church building, we built for six months without making any payments or signing a loan agreement. How did that happen? Because I gave my word to the company that gave us the money with which to start building.

I said, "I give you my word. We will repay you." My word was good. I was true to my word; I had the reputation of being a man of integrity whose word can be trusted.

What are you saying to God today? What promises have you made? What promises are you making? And more important, what promises are you keeping?

What are you saying to your spouse? What promises are you making or have you made? More important, what promises are you keeping?

What are you saying to your children, your friends, your co-workers? What promises have you made? What promises are you keeping?

Don't Forget

Adhere and *adhesive* come from the same root word. Stick to your promises like superglue! Don't abandon your promises or forget them.

You are to your spouse what your spouse can trust you to be. You are no better than the promises you make and don't break. "I forgot" is no excuse.

It doesn't matter what you say; it matters how you keep—adhere to, follow through on, perform—the promises you make.

"I promise I'll never do that again."

"I promise to do better."

"I promise I'll make the changes I need to make."

When you don't follow through and keep those promises, you make matters worse. It would be better if you never made the promises in the first place!

Trust and promises go together.

It's very difficult for a woman to submit to someone she doesn't trust. And it's very difficult for a woman to trust a man who makes promises and then breaks them.

The opposite is also true. It is very difficult for a man to cover his wife—to provide for her, protect her, love her as Christ loves the church—if that man doesn't know where she is! You can't "cover" what you can't find!

Trust and promises go together.

Integrity is when your life matches your word. If you say with your mouth, "I'm the best," but you live out behavior that falls into the category of "worst," you destroy integrity.

Don't Hide Your Friendships

"He's just a friend." Well, why don't you invite him over so he can meet your husband and you three can be friends together?

"She's just somebody I met on the phone and enjoy talking with." Well, why don't you introduce her to your wife so your wife can talk to her on the phone and enjoy getting to know her?

Once you're married, you no longer have the right to have exclusive friendships with people of the opposite sex.

There's absolutely no room for a third person in your marriage. Marriage is made for two—male and female, husband and wife.

I know a man who developed an innocent friendship with a woman in his church. There wasn't anything sexual between them. He enjoyed the company of this woman. She could make him laugh, she'd listen to his old worn-out stories, and she'd serve him a good cup of coffee and a nice piece of pie when he stopped by her house. He found her easy to talk to; she was always pleasant and cheerful.

The friendship developed over a few months. At Christmas that year, he bought her a dress as a present. He had it delivered a week before Christmas because he needed to have surgery over the Christmas holiday.

While he was in surgery, his wife answered the phone to find that this woman was calling her husband to thank him for the dress. Now, his wife knew that her husband knew this woman from the church. She knew that her husband had talked to this woman on occasion. But she had no idea that her husband had developed a friendship with this woman to the point that he had bought her a dress!

Well, when that husband came out of surgery, there was his wife ready to help wheel his bed out of the recovery room into a regular hospital room. She let him know right then and there that he was not about to have that kind of friendship with another woman. She told him that he was going to put an end to that friendship—and as you might suspect, the man is lying there on the gurney, just out of surgery, weak as a kitten, and no place to go. He had to agree!

When he got home a couple of days before Christmas, he was greeted by his wife wearing the dress he had given to the other woman! He never asked her how she got it.

Jesus said this about adultery:

> *You have heard that it was said to those of old, "You shall not commit adultery." But I say to you that whoever looks at a woman to lust for her has already committed adultery with her in his heart.* (Matthew 5:27–28)

Adultery does not just suddenly emerge one day. The *idea* of adultery begins in the mind—in the imagination, in the fantasy realm—long before it is acted out in real behavior. Adultery can begin very innocently. It can begin with an innocent friend-ship—the enjoyment of a person's company, a delight in the way a person treats you, a friendly conversation that leaves you feeling good about yourself. The more that friendship develops, the more likely it is to be laced with a little flirtation and a little teasing. And if that flirtation and teasing go on for a while, one or both of those "just friends" are going to start to imagine what it might be like to hold that person or kiss that person. Pretty soon, lust takes over.

If a person gets into the habit of acting on lust, then it takes far less "friendship" and far less flirtation and teasing to get to the point of actually committing adultery. If a person has a string of extramarital or premarital affairs, lust has already taken root. The person can go from "look" to "touch" to "sex" very quickly.

Jesus said, in essence, that adultery isn't just an act. It's a pro-cess that begins long before the act. If you are keeping a friend-ship secret from your spouse, ask yourself why. Ask yourself where you are secretly hoping this friendship will go. Face up to the fact that you may have allowed a seed of adultery to be planted into your imagination.

I recently heard about a woman who had been married for about ten years when she innocently sat next to a man at a Little League softball game. She and this man both had children on the team. She was a good listener, and this man opened up to her and told her that his wife had left him and he was struggling in his attempts to be both mom and dad to his two children.

The woman felt sorry for this man. Even though she didn't cook regularly for her husband—always claiming that he was a better cook than she was—she found herself making a casserole to take to this man. When she got to his house, she discovered he was wearing a rumpled shirt. He apologized for his appearance and said he didn't know how to iron. She took home a few shirts to iron for him. When she delivered them, he asked if he could take her to lunch as a "thank you."

It all sounds innocent and friendly, right? It sounds as if this woman was just being a good Christian friend, right? That's the way it started.

106

A few more shirts, a few more casseroles, a few more thank-you lunches, a few more telephone conversations, and a big-time conflict resulted in this woman's relationship with her husband. He had no tolerance for a wife who ironed another man's shirts and didn't iron his, who cooked for another man but wouldn't cook for him, or who went out on the town to lunch with another man.

Don't invite this kind of conflict into your life. If a person tells you his or her troubles, you can listen and then offer to pray...and then walk away or say that you'll discuss with your spouse how the two of you might be of help. Recommend a few delis or take-out restaurants the person might call. Remind him or her that the dry cleaner will iron shirts for very little money. Don't get involved in doing for a person without your spouse's full consent.

Break Off the Friendship That You Can't Share with Your Spouse

Jesus said,

> If your right eye causes you to sin, pluck it out and cast it from you; for it is more profitable for you that one of your members perish, than for your whole body to be cast into hell. And if your right hand causes you to sin, cut it off and cast it from you; for it is more profitable for you that one of your members perish, than for your whole body to be cast into hell. (Matthew 5:29–30)

Now, Jesus knew that if people had a difficult time saying no to a lustful fantasy and letting go of an "imagination affair," people certainly wouldn't be able to let go of an eye or an arm. He wasn't advocating physical maiming; He was making a point by going to the extreme. He was saying that if there's a secret you are holding about a person of the opposite sex other than your spouse, you need to get rid of that fantasy. If you have allowed a friendship to develop with a person of the opposite sex, get rid of that friendship. Cut it off. End it. Put a stop to it. Pluck out the problem and get rid of it.

A couple decades ago there was a popular song that had this refrain: "There must be fifty ways to leave a lover." That song never mentioned, however, the first and easiest way to say no to a lover: say "no" to the very idea of a lover the first moment that idea pops into your mind!

Get rid of the secret. Don't allow it to become something valuable or sacred to you. That secret can grow until it is more valuable to you than telling the truth to your spouse.

Don't make a promise to keep something secret from your spouse. The moment you do that, you are driving a wedge between you and your spouse.

Do ask. Do tell. What you reveal is what can be healed, forgiven, discussed, restored, and improved!

9

Keep Learning How to Be Married

Marriage Commandment #6:
Thou Shalt Grow in Your Understanding

❖❖❖

Wisdom is the principal thing; therefore get wisdom. And in all your getting, get understanding.
—Proverbs 4:7

I once met a couple who had been married for twenty-five years and then, apparently without warning or any outward signs of conflict, got divorced. One day I had the opportunity to ask the former wife what had happened in their relationship. She said with sadness in her voice, "We woke up after twenty-five years and admitted to each other that we really didn't know each other. We had each gone our separate ways early in the marriage, and over time we became strangers to each other."

> You must continue to "study" each other.

How sad...and how preventable.

Married couples need to face this reality: you must continue to "study" each other and grow in your understanding of each other.

One of the most famous passages in the New Testament related to male and female relationships is found in the apostle Paul's letter to Titus:

> But as for you [Titus], *speak the things which are proper for sound doctrine: that the older men be sober, reverent, temperate, sound in faith, in love, in patience; the older women likewise, that they be reverent in behavior, not slanderers, not given to much wine, teachers of good things; that they admonish the young women to love their husbands, to love their children, to be discreet, chaste, homemakers, good, obedient to their own husbands, that the word of God may not be blasphemed.* (Titus 2:1–5)

Why does Titus need to speak to adult men to show love and patience? Because men who are geared to take dominion and to exhibit "rulership" need to learn how to temper their dominion and rulership with love and patience!

Why do the older women need to *admonish* the young women to love their husbands and to love their children? Why do they need to admonish the young women to be discreet, chaste, homemakers, good, and obedient to their own husbands? Because women who are geared toward fruitfulness and dominion from their creation need to *learn* how to display these behaviors and character qualities in their relationship to their husbands.

Becoming a good wife or husband is a learning process.

Becoming a good wife or husband is a learning process.

Many people believe that when they become adults, they will automatically know how to have a good marriage. That isn't the case. Age has nothing to do with learning how to be married. A person who is fifty and who has never been married has just as much learning to do as a person who is twenty-one.

Many people believe that when they submit their lives to the Lord, confess their sins, and are saved, they automatically know how to live the Christian life to the fullest, including how to have a good marriage. That isn't the case. We each need to learn how to walk in faith before the Lord. We also need to learn how to live in right relationship with other people, including how to have a good marital relationship.

If you don't learn God's way for marriage, you will learn *some-body's* way. It may be the way of your father or mother, or your aunt or uncle, or your grandfather or grandmother, or the leaders of your culture. And whatever you learn from a source other than the Bible is something you are going to have to unlearn if you truly want to have a good marriage.

By "learn" I'm not talking about formal training or teaching; I'm not talking about having a long talk that is instructional. I'm talking about learning by watching the behavior of others you respect and admire. Most of us learn our attitudes, beliefs, and behaviors by watching others.

You can't, however, be listening to your Uncle Bubba telling you, "You got to keep your woman under your thumb."

You can't be listening to your auntie telling you, "You can't trust no man. You've got to set something aside for yourself first."

You have to learn from people who know what they are talking about and who are basing their lives on God's Word.

The Bible promises that you can find what you are seeking if you go to God with your questions. Jesus made this very clear: *"Ask, and it will be given to you; seek, and you will find; knock, and it will be opened to you"* (Matthew 7:7).

If you don't know how to have a good marriage...

If you don't know how to be a good husband...

If you don't know how to be a good wife...

Ask God! Seek out God's principles about marriage in the Bible. Knock on the door of the church that can help you by teaching you God's commandments, and take advantage of all that the church offers to help you build up your marriage.

When I got married more than twenty years ago, I had an incomplete understanding of marriage and, more specifically, an incomplete understanding of *my* marriage. I didn't think about my wife, Pam, being one flesh with me or our reflecting the nature of God. I thought, *Oooh, I have a fine wife. I can hardly wait to get home to be with her.* I thought, *I'm the man; my wife ought to do what I say.* I saw my wife the way I chose to see her and the way other people had told me I should see her. As a result, I never spoke to her what God said about her or what God said about us as a married couple. I spoke to her the truth according to Darrell, not the truth according to God.

Now the only place where you can go to find the truth according to God is the Bible. If you want your life and your marriage to reflect God's nature, you need to go to your Bible to find out what God says you are to be like. In the Bible you will find the character qualities of a godly person and a godly relationship. In the Bible you will find the traits and functions of a godly husband and a godly wife.

Dwell with Understanding

Peter wrote, *"Husbands, likewise, dwell with them* [your wives] *with understanding"* (1 Peter 3:7).

Husband, get some understanding about your wife and your marriage. Learn from God's Word. Get some understanding about how God sees your wife and her ministry.

When a woman marries, the gifts that God has imparted to her do not evaporate. That's true for her natural gifts and her intelligence as well as for her spiritual gifts. If your wife was a prophetess before she got married, she still has that gift of prophecy. It's up to you as her husband to give that gift direction and an opportunity to grow, flourish, and bear fruit in the kingdom of God.

Husband, get some understanding.

Part of the understanding you need to gain about your wife is the understanding that your wife has been given gifts to *help* you. Many wives are more sensitive and intuitive than their husbands; your wife's sensitivity and intuition can help you. Early in my marriage, I shut myself off from many of my wife's attempts to help me. She has a spiritual gift of discernment, but when she tried to warn me or encourage me in certain situations, I took her advice as "telling me what to do." So, being a macho man, I rebelled against that and didn't hear her. Who lost in that deal? I did.

When I got to the point that I recognized this as a gift functioning in her according to the power of the Holy Spirit, I opened my mind and my heart to receive what my wife had to say to me. When I did, I was greatly helped in my ministry. My ministry became more effective, more focused, and more powerful. Who won in that deal? I did. She did. The church did. The unbelievers who came to Christ did.

My wife is the co-pastor of our church. She's the co-pastor because I asked God what role *He* wanted her to take in our church, and He revealed to me that He wanted her to be co-pastor. That's the role God had for her not only as a woman, but also as my wife. That's the role God designed for her to be of greatest "help" to me. She is my "helpmeet" not only at home, but also in the church.

Most godly men are concerned primarily about understanding who God has called them to be. They listen intently when God tells them what He wants them to do, where He wants them to go, and how He wants them to function in ministry. They never or rarely stop to ask, "God, what do You want for my wife?"

Abraham, the father of all who have faith, heard God say this to him: *"I am Almighty God; walk before Me and be blameless. And I will make My covenant between Me and you, and will multiply you exceedingly"* (Genesis 17:1–2). Abram fell on his face at those words, and God went on, saying:

> *As for Me, behold, My covenant is with you, and you shall be a father of many nations. No longer shall your name be called Abram, but your name shall be Abraham; for I have made you a father of many nations. I will make you exceedingly fruitful; and I will make nations of you, and kings shall come from you. And I will establish My covenant between Me and you and your descendants after you in their generations, for an everlasting covenant, to be God to you and your descendants after you. Also I give to you*

and your descendants after you the land in which you are
a stranger, all the land of Canaan, as an everlasting posses-
sion; and I will be their God.　　　　　(Genesis 17:4–8)

What a powerful call to Abraham! But as you continue to read
God's directives to Abraham, you eventually come to this statement:

As for Sarai your wife, you shall not call her name Sarai, but
Sarah shall be her name. And I will bless her and also give
you a son by her; then I will bless her, and she shall be a
mother of nations; kings of peoples shall be from her.
　　　　　　　　　　　　　　　　　　　　(vv. 15–16)

God not only called Abraham to be the father of many nations,
but He also called Sarah to be the mother of nations, and He
revealed her new identity to *Abraham*. Abraham, in turn, was the
one who spoke Sarah's identity to her.

What has God said to you, husband, about the identity, role,
and purpose for your wife's life on this earth? I'm not talking
about what you *hope* her identity, role, and purpose will be; or
what your culture or background has said her identity, role, and
purpose will be; or what someone who is a parent, friend, or
coworker has said her identity, role, and purpose will be. Have
you asked God what He says about your wife?

Get understanding! Get understanding about how God sees
your wife. Get God's definition for who she is to be, what role
she is to fill, and what ministry purpose God has for her on this
earth. Then, encourage her in it! Don't nag. Don't coerce. Instead,
encourage your wife to become all that God has designed and
prepared and called her to be!

Stop to think for a moment how Abraham's thinking must have
changed after God spoke to him. He suddenly saw himself as a
father of many nations, an exceedingly fruitful man, the forerun-
ner of kings, the possessor of a land. He also saw his wife as a
woman who was blessed, a mother of nations.

How we see ourselves becomes how we behave. What you
think you will be is how you direct your life, so that what you

114

think is what you become. The same is true for the way you behave toward others. If you see others as being blessed, forgiven, fruitful, and honored by God, then you treat them as God sees them.

By your attitude, your words, and your behavior, you help them become all that God has designed them to be. This is especially true, husband, for your wife.

If you see your wife as a prophetess called and gifted by God, you aren't going to have any trouble relating to her as a prophet. Her gift of prophecy isn't going to threaten you or cause you to diminish in self-worth. Rather, her gift of prophecy will be regarded by you as something that blesses you as her husband, blesses your family, blesses your church, and blesses this world.

If you see your wife as blessed and honored by God with intelligence and ability to succeed in a particular task or job, and if you see her called by God to pursue that particular task or job in a particular way, then you aren't going to have any problem with her fulfilling who she has been created and called to be.

Remind Yourself of the Basics—Often!

It's not enough that you know the principles for a good marriage at the outset. You need to remind yourselves of those principles *often*. Pamela and I have found in marriage counseling that we often need to repeat and repeat certain principles—and there's good reason for this. Marriage is a twenty-four-hours-a-day, seven-days-a-week relationship. Because marriage is intended by God to be a permanent relationship that is continuously renewed, we need to remind ourselves continuously of those principles that we hold to be vital for a good marriage.

Marriages are sometimes under attack for a "season." Some marriages, it seems, are under almost continual attack. No sooner do you get through one crisis than another one pops up. No sooner do you think you get one issue settled than another one raises its ugly head.

• Keep learning from God's Word.

• Keep learning how to guard your own heart against temptation.

• Keep learning how to be more sensitive to each other.

The more you keep learning, the more you'll grow in understanding and wisdom. The wiser you become about your spouse and about your marriage, the more you will be able to prevent most conflicts and quickly resolve conflicts that do arise.

10

Build Your Friendship

Marriage Commandment #7:
Thou Shalt Be Friends

A friend loves at all times.
—Proverbs 17:17

My wife, Pamela, is my best friend. And I feel confident she would tell you that I am her best friend. Not only that, but we are friends in the Lord; we are "brother and sister" in Christ Jesus. Friendship and faith go hand in hand in our marriage. I strongly believe that genuine friendship and faith are at the core of every good marriage I know.

Many people go into marriage thinking that sex is the basis for a good marriage. Their viewpoint is this: "The better the sex, the better the marriage; the more passionate and frequent the sex, the stronger the marriage bond."

Let me assure you that if you and your spouse do not become *friends,* you will eventually stop enjoying sex. There is a bond of affection and esteem that is vitally important to the sustaining of a good sexual relationship. Affection and esteem can and often do generate a good sexual relationship; sexual intimacy gives expression to the affection and esteem that is already felt. This doesn't always work in reverse—a

> Friendship and faith go hand in hand in our marriage.

117

good sexual relationship may or may not generate affection and esteem. People often "use" each other for sexual gratification, and, in the end, those who do this esteem the sexual partner less, not more. I've met people who told me they didn't even *like* the person with whom they were having sex. They were merely using that person to meet their physical need and desire for sex.

I see married people all the time who don't act friendly to each other. They are cold, distant, aloof. Their words have a biting, cutting, sarcastic, or disgusted edge to them. I want to shout at them: "Act friendly! Become friends!"

Build a Strong "Association"

What is it that friends do for and with each other?

Friends spend time together.

Friends do things together.

Friends laugh and cry together.

A friend is a person who is attached to another person by affection or esteem. A friend is not hostile, but rather has the same mind. A friend is a favored companion.

Friends do not hurt one another. A man doesn't launch abusive words on his friend or call up his friend to say, "I wish you were dead." The contrary is true! A man speaks good words to his friend. He seeks to do good to his friend. The more he values the friendship, the more good words and good deeds he is likely to say and do!

Friends "associate." They are on the same side. They stand together, rather than stand in opposition to each other.

Not all opposition is outward or explosive. Opposition is also manifested in the form of disassociation or competition.

Disassociation

A husband or wife who is strongly opposed to cooperating is likely to walk away from the relationship. He may not physically move out of the house, but he'll move out of the relationship.

He may become involved with another person emotionally and perhaps even sexually. He may become "distant," silent, withdrawn, and even depressed. He may spend more and more time at work, away from the family, or with friends. What is true for husbands here is also true for wives. Wives who disassociate from their husbands often choose to spend more time talking to their friends, mother, or children than to a spouse; they may choose to withdraw sexually or to envelop themselves in silence.

Competition

Husbands and wives are not to be in competition; rather, they are to be in cooperation. Husbands and wives who start competing with each other rarely stop competing. They are continually vying for the limelight, the applause, the recognition, the rewards. The husband or wife who has a competitive spirit with his or her spouse is rarely a satisfied, joyful, fulfilled person. Rather, the competitive spouse nearly always feels put upon, put down, or put out; the competitive spouse feels neglected, "diminished," and overlooked. The end result is a person who is bitter, frustrated, angry, and generally dissatisfied with all of life.

The Bible takes a strong stance against these forms of opposition: disassociation and competition. The Bible stands for unity and love among believers in Christ Jesus. The Bible stands for marriage, family, and reconciliation. The Bible stands for being "one" in Christ—one faith, one Lord, one Word, one commitment, one in Christ. (See Galatians 3:28.)

The Bible tells us that we are to

> walk worthy of the calling with which you were called, with all lowliness and gentleness, with longsuffering, bearing with one another in love, endeavoring to keep the unity of the Spirit in the bond of peace. There is one body and one Spirit, just as you were called in one hope of your calling; one Lord, one faith, one baptism; one God and Father of all, who is above all, and through all, and in you all.
>
> (Ephesians 4:1–6)

119

Refuse to Play the Blame Game

Satan will always point out something to you concerning your spouse that will make it difficult for you to forgive your spouse. When you listen to his voice instead of God's, you fuel your spouse's actions against you because the devil will cause you to react in a way that is inflammatory. Usually that reaction is in the form of accusation or blame.

Don't Accuse

Accusation is saying, "You are a lousy person." You can drop any negative adjective in place of the word *lousy,* and you have an accusation. "You are a mean person." "You are a sinful person." "You are an awful person."

You may be speaking the truth, but your spouse is going to perceive what you say as an accusation, and an accusation will inflame the very behavior you are trying to confront. Saying "You are a wicked person for seeing that woman behind my back" is only going to cause your spouse to try to justify his behavior and argue and get defensive. In the end, what you say will drive him right back into her arms. In saying "You are a terrible house-keeper," you are going to cause your wife to feel hurt, dejected, angry, and defensive. In the end, to get back at you, she's going to do even less housekeeping.

Don't accuse the person. Address the issue. Say to your spouse, "I want to talk about..." Then, don't make the subject your spouse's character, nature, background, parentage, or appearance. Talk about the specific incident of *behavior,* the specific problem you perceive, or the specific pattern of responding that is a problem to you.

This is important not only in the way you speak to your spouse, but also to the way you think.

If you continually label your spouse with negative terms and phrases, you are going to think about your spouse in a negative way. Before long, you won't even be able to think a positive thought toward your spouse. You will find yourself responding to your spouse in the negative way you have been thinking. And if your spouse didn't know what you were thinking by reading your mind, he or she is going to know loud and clear what you think by the way you behave.

Avoid Blaming

Blaming is saying, "You are the cause of something that has caused a problem." That problem might be in you; it might be the problem of the way you feel. Blaming your spouse is saying, "You made me cry," "You made me get upset," "You made me angry," "You made me act that way," or "You made me say those mean things."

Blaming is also placing fault for a mutual problem at your spouse's feet. It's saying, "We never have any money because you spend it on...," or "We don't have any friends because you always act like a jerk."

When you blame your spouse for a problem that the two of you are mutually experiencing, you are diminishing the value or worth of your spouse. You are saying that your spouse isn't sufficient to meet your needs, to provide for you, to nurture you, to protect you, to love you. You are saying your spouse can't satisfy you. The spouse who hears blame gives up; he or she doesn't feel like trying, doesn't feel any motivation to make changes, and doesn't have the energy to think about improving or growing or developing.

Again, if *you* are blaming your spouse for all your problems, you are failing to take the responsibility *you* need to take before God and in your relationship. In the end, too much blame will destroy any regard or respect you have for your spouse in your own mind.

Blame is one of the deadliest things that can ever infect a marriage. If a child dies in an accident and one spouse blames the other for that death, you can pretty much predict that marriage is over. If a family goes bankrupt and one spouse blames the other totally for the financial failure, you can pretty much predict that

> Blame is one of the deadliest things that can ever infect a marriage.

marriage is doomed. Why? Because the faults of the spouse become so enlarged by blame and the extent of the consequences have caused such pain that you won't even *think* about forgiving your spouse. The conflict between you will continue to grow and never be resolved, and, in the end, you'll be worn out from "trying to make it work" when, in reality, you never stopped the problem in your own mind that is keeping your marriage from moving forward.

Don't blame your spouse. Recognize the problems, and do what you can to help, build up, and encourage your spouse. Point out his or her good qualities. Do your part to help energize and motivate your spouse. Offer suggestions that your *spouse* finds helpful. Do the things that your *spouse* finds beneficial to his total well-being. And, above all, choose to think the best of your spouse.

Believe for the best.

Pray for the best.

Expect the best.

Encourage the best.

Hope for the best.

Have faith for the best.

Stay focused on the *best* your spouse can be and the *best* your marriage can be. Blame and accusation are nothing but negative fuel to conflict. They are huge obstacles in the way of forgiveness.

Friends Give Generously

Friends give generously to each other. Be generous in what you give to your spouse!

In the course of counseling couples about marriage, my wife and I have found that, nine times out of ten, people approach marriage with great expectations about what their future spouse is going to do for them. They are eagerly anticipating all the ways in which their spouse is going to help them, "do" for them, love them, and so forth. Very few individuals approach marriage saying, "Here's what I am looking forward to doing for my future spouse."

It's time you start thinking, *What do I have to give to my spouse? What can I give to my spouse? What should I give to my spouse?*

Rather than ask, "What can my spouse do for me to make me happy?" we need to ask, "What can I do for my spouse to add to my spouse's happiness?"

"But," you may say, "I don't know how to make my spouse happy."

I doubt that's true. You knew enough about how to make that person happy in order to get that person to marry you. If you have any doubts about how to make your spouse happy, ask your spouse. Make it your personal goal to find out how to please your spouse and give pleasure to your spouse. Find out what your spouse enjoys and what gives joy to your spouse.

In many cases, the biblical advice to "do unto others as you would have them do unto you" is good. Jesus said, *"Whatever you want men [or literally, another person] to do to you, do also to them"* (Matthew 7:12).

There are some things that we all want. Everybody likes to be treated with kindness, courtesy, and respect. Everybody likes to be pampered and appreciated and thanked. Everybody enjoys being rewarded with praise. But, at other times, your spouse may not want or enjoy exactly what you want and enjoy.

I recently heard about a woman who did not enjoy surprises. Too many times in her life, surprises had been bad surprises. Her husband, who loved surprises, thought surely his wife would enjoy being surprised, and at first he was hurt that she didn't at all enjoy receiving what he enjoyed giving. He had to learn *how* to surprise his wife in a way in which she could thoroughly enjoy the surprise. His solution was to work on a series of "clues" that let her know something good was coming, and that he was going to lead her step by step to it. She enjoyed that!

Give What You Want to Receive

Do you stop talking to your spouse because you don't like the way your spouse talks to you?

Do you get angry with your spouse because your spouse shows anger to you?

Do you shut out your spouse because you think your spouse is shutting you out?

Do what it is that you want your spouse to do. Turn the record over. If your spouse speaks to you in a tone of voice you don't like, speak back to your spouse in the way you want your spouse to talk to you. If your spouse shows anger to you, show kindness and gentleness to your spouse. If your spouse shuts you out, don't give your spouse the silent treatment; speak to your spouse and reach out to him or her.

"But what if I'm right and my spouse really is wrong?"

It doesn't matter.

If you take the position of "I'm right, you're wrong," you are going to be in conflict; and the more you stick to that position, the more hurt and wounded you will end up. On the other hand, if you say to your spouse, "My perception about this may be off, but I'm hurting. I need to talk to you about something," you are setting yourself up for resolution of a conflict. There's hope and healing in that position.

"I'm right and you're wrong" is an adversarial position. It's a position that turns quickly to accusation and blame.

Once conflict escalates, it's very difficult for two people to recall what brought them together. All they see are the things that should bring them to a divorce court. They no longer see the positive traits that attracted them in the first place. They see only the negative traits that are now something they want to escape.

Choose to Live Together in Peace

Friends find a way to relate to each other in harmony. They "yield" to each other. In traveling the freeway of conflict, they choose to take the exit marked "Peace."

Jesus said, *"Agree with your adversary quickly"* (Matthew 5:25).

Let me give you an example of this.

A husband comes home to find his wife on the phone. She doesn't greet him. He feels unloved and overlooked. He resents the time she spends on the phone. And he reacts.

HUSBAND: I wish you'd get off that phone. Every time I come home you're on the phone. You're probably talking about me to your friends—telling them stuff they don't need to know.

WIFE: Don't tell me who I can talk to or how long I can talk on the phone. I pay the phone bill, too.

HUSBAND: Well, I bought the phone.

WIFE: Why are you getting so upset about the phone? You come in here a half hour after you told me you'd be here. What did you think—that I'd be sitting her just waiting for you to walk through that door?

HUSBAND: I don't know why you have to be on the phone. You could be cleaning up this messy house instead of running your mouth to this one and that one. Who were you talking to, anyway? You should be talking to me instead of talking about me to whomever it is you're talking to all the time.

WIFE: Well, I would talk to you, but you never listen to me. You never *want* to talk.

HUSBAND: That's the problem. When I talk, you don't listen. You just run your mouth, and you never let me get a word in edgewise. I get sick of hearing all that you don't think I am or all that you don't think I'm doing.

WIFE: Well, the reason I come at you like that is because I never know when I'm going to get another chance.

HUSBAND: You'd better shut up right now. I'm sick of your mouth.

That's pretty much when the husband stomps off or gets abusive. The problem has escalated from a wife being on the phone to a major conflict!

But let's consider how this might be resolved *quickly.*

HUSBAND: I wish you'd get off that phone. Every time I come home you're on the phone. You're probably talking about me to your friends—telling them stuff they don't need to know.

WIFE: I'm sorry, sweetheart. I didn't know my being on the phone bothered you. Now that I know, I won't make phone calls when I know it's about time for you to come home. I'll do my best to give you my undivided attention because you're my number-one friend.

HUSBAND: I just want to be with you, talk to you, and have you there for me.

WIFE: And I want to be there for you.

At that point...well, who knows what can happen behind closed doors at that point!

See how easily the problem is defused.

Of course, the wife needs to go ahead and do what she said. She needs to stay off the phone when it's about time for her husband to come home. That doesn't mean she can never be on the phone when he shows up at home. It means she chooses not to always be on the phone when he gets home.

It's the repeated, habitual, "normal" conduct that gives rise to conflict.

Usually, it's not the isolated incident that causes conflict in marriage. It's the repeated, habitual, "normal" conduct that gives rise to conflict. It's the bad habits, the frequent put-downs, the prolonged absences, and the routine, hurtful remarks.

What's the best way to keep one incident from becoming a bad habit? Deal with it the first time as an incident. If you don't deal with it then, deal with it the second time it happens because then you know the "repeat" button has been pushed. And if you don't deal with it then, by all means deal with it the third time because by then it's a "new habit." Don't let it go on. If you do, it will become ingrained in the behavior of the person, and it will become a part of the way you relate to each other in your marriage.

What Kind of Friend Are You?

Take a look in the mirror and ask yourself, "What kind of friend am I to my spouse?" Then ask, "What have I done today to help nurture that friendship?"

No matter how good a friend you are, you can always be a better friend.

11

Never Stop Forgiving

Marriage Commandment #8:
Thou Shalt Forgive and Forgive and Forgive

Forgive, and you will be forgiven.
—Luke 6:37

Peter, one of Jesus' closest disciples, came to Him one day and said, *"Lord, how often shall my brother sin against me, and I forgive him? Up to seven times?"* (Matthew 18:21).

The question Peter asked is a question that most married people ask! Some spouses nearly wear out their marriage with their mistakes and sins. Every marriage has opportunities for forgiveness—generally on a daily basis!

The reason forgiveness is so important is that marriage doesn't involve two perfect people. There is no such thing as a "perfect" marriage because, in order for it to be perfect, it would have to be the union of two perfect people—and those people don't exist on this earth.

People make mistakes. Even if you are a Christian, you are going to make mistakes. And we're responsible for our mistakes. But our *response* to a person who makes mistakes can also be a mistake if we aren't careful. We're responsible to God for the response we make to people who make mistakes, including our spouses. So our concern must be twofold: not only what we do that is in error, but also how we respond to those closest to us who err.

You need to forgive because you need to be forgiven.

Jesus replied to Peter,

> *I do not say to you, up to seven times, but up to seventy times seven. Therefore the kingdom of heaven is like a certain king who wanted to settle accounts with his servants. And when he had begun to settle accounts, one was brought to him who owed him ten thousand talents. But as he was not able to pay, his master commanded that he be sold, with his wife and children and all that he had, and that payment be made. The servant therefore fell down before him, saying, "Master, have patience with me, and I will pay you all." Then the master of that servant was moved with compassion, released him, and forgave him the debt. But that servant went out and found one of his fellow servants who owed him a hundred denarii; and he laid hands on him and took him by the throat, saying, "Pay me what you owe!" So his fellow servant fell down at his feet and begged him, saying, "Have patience with me, and I will pay you all." And he would not, but went and threw him into prison till he should pay the debt. So when his fellow servants saw what had been done, they were very grieved, and came and told their master all that had been done. Then his master, after he had called him, said to him, "You wicked servant! I forgave you all that debt because you begged me. Should you not also have had compassion on your fellow servant, just as I had pity on you?" And his master was angry, and delivered him to the torturers until he should pay all that was due to him. So My heavenly Father also will do to you if each of you, from his heart, does not forgive his brother his trespasses.* (Matthew 18:22–35)

I feel certain that Peter was stunned when Jesus told him he needed to forgive those who sinned against him seventy times seven. Peter thought he was being generous in suggesting forgiveness seven times!

130

Imagine how stunned he was when Jesus placed such heavy consequences on a failure to forgive—and when Jesus cited the great discrepancy that needed to be forgiven!

How Big Is Your Own Sin?

The servant in this parable owed *"ten thousand talents."* That's a huge debt. In today's money, that debt would have amounted to about ten million dollars. But in a way that would have been more readily understood at the time, the debt would have been equal to the wages for about sixty million days of common labor! In other words, it was a debt that could never be paid in a person's lifetime. The king graciously heard the servant's plea and had compassion on him and released him from the debt.

Jesus was saying, of course, that this is what our heavenly Father does on our behalf. No matter how many good works we do or how fine an attitude we have, we cannot do enough to "earn" God's forgiveness of our sin nature. We deserve to be thrown into bondage and suffer the consequences for our sin. It is only by the mercy and compassion of God that we are forgiven and released from sin.

The second servant owed a hundred denarii, which is about sixteen to eighteen dollars—an amount that could have been paid in less than three weeks of common labor. The ratio between the two amounts owed is about six hundred thousand to one!

Yet the servant who owed the most leaned on the servant who owed the least and demanded payment, even when this second servant begged him to have patience.

The master heard about this and said to the first servant, "You wicked servant! I forgave you. You should have had compassion on your fellow servant." The master then turned him over to the torturer.

What does this say to us about marriage?

How many spouses do you know who are hung up on the "small stuff" in life? They get upset if their husband drops a shirt on the floor or fails to put down the toilet seat. They get upset if their wife buys a new blouse at the mall or spends a few minutes on the phone with her mother.

Get real. Take a look at your own life. What has your heavenly Father forgiven in your life? How is your heavenly Father patient with you, forgiving you day in and day out for all those things that you say you are going to do and want to do, but that you fail to do? How is your heavenly Father merciful to you even when you ignore Him, disappoint Him, overlook Him in favor of other things or people, or break His commandments?

No person keeps all the commandments of God at all times, in all situations, with maximum consistency and effort. The Bible says clearly, *"All have sinned and fall short of the glory of God"* (Romans 3:23).

If God is patient with you, then surely He expects you to be patient with your spouse. He expects you to forgive your spouse. He expects you to have just a small portion of the vast mercy, love, and compassion He has for your spouse, and to extend kindness and forgiveness to your spouse even when your spouse "trespasses" against you.

What Forgiveness Is and Isn't

To trespass means to walk on the flowers in your garden. It means to get in your space. It means to infringe upon your personal agenda. It means to use some of your stuff. It means to "step" on you, sometimes unintentionally and sometimes intentionally.

Forgiveness does not mean that you ignore what is happening. It doesn't mean that you sweep the debt under the rug or that you shrug your shoulders and walk off in frustration saying, "Oh, well." To the contrary—forgiveness is an active process. Forgiveness means that you confront and state what is happening, but you do so *with a spirit of forgiveness.* Forgiveness is saying, "You are trespassing on my garden. You are hurting me. You are frustrating me. You are irritating me. You are ignoring me. You are 'using' me in

Forgiveness is an active process.

ways that I don't appreciate being used. You are saying things that cause me emotional pain."

Note that the master "settled accounts" with his servant. He didn't see the debt on the books and say, "I'll just ignore that." No, he had the servant brought to him, and he did so for a purpose—to see if the servant would acknowledge the debt and ask for mercy.

For the same purpose, we are to confront those who cause us emotional pain or do us harm—to give them an opportunity to be forgiven, to call attention to what is happening so the debt doesn't mount up to an even greater sum, and to attempt to put an end to the behavior that is offensive or sinful. We need to give other people an opportunity to repent, to be forgiven, and to change their ways—for their sake as well as for our sake and the sake of our marriage.

But we must do so always, always, *always* with forgiveness in our mind. We cannot come to a confrontation about sin with the intent of punishing that sin or harming the other person. We must come to the confrontation with an attitude of forgiveness, having a sharp awareness that we have been forgiven by our heavenly Father for far more serious and consequential sins.

If we do not come to a settling of accounts in this way, we put ourselves in grave danger. We find ourselves wallowing in our own sin. We heap even more guilt on our own souls because we hold an attitude of unforgiveness toward our spouse.

The Process of Forgiveness

So how do we approach forgiveness and confrontation about sin in a godly manner?

First, know that you *can* forgive. I believe that God gives a special grace to Christians to forgive. They are capable of forgiving because they know they have been forgiven. It is especially important for Christian spouses to be able to openly forgive their unsaved spouses, for in doing so they model forgiveness and give a powerful witness for Jesus Christ.

You *can* forgive.

See Your Spouse as God Sees Your Spouse

Learn to see how God sees your spouse. Before your spouse is your spouse, your spouse is a child of God. God loves your spouse, wants to extend mercy and forgiveness to your spouse, and desires to see your spouse become more and more like Jesus.

I don't care what my wife, Pamela, has done to make me angry; if I want to please God and if I desire my marriage to be strong, I have to go to Pamela and say, "Pamela, I forgive you." I must forgive her from my heart because she is first and foremost a child of God, and *He* desires to forgive her.

It's hard to hold something against a spouse whom you forgive.

It's hard to be free of the "feelings" associated with a problem, or to get beyond a problem, if you don't forgive your spouse.

Admit Your Own Sin

Face up to your own sin. Recognize that you have faults and weaknesses. Recognize that you are likely trespassing against your spouse just as much as your spouse is trespassing against you. It's not the "seriousness" of the sin that matters before God; sin is sin before God. Fornication, murder, anger, and gossip are all on the same list. Sin is sin. Sin is like a stain of black ink on a white suit. It doesn't matter if that stain is the size of a dime or fifteen inches in diameter—the suit is ruined all the same.

If you don't think you have any sin in the matter, then you need to face up to the fact that you are in error and ask God to reveal to you your sin—not just in one situation or circumstance, but in the prevailing nature of your heart. The Bible tells us, *"If we say that we have no sin, we deceive ourselves, and the truth is not in us"* (1 John 1:8).

Ask God for Forgiveness

As we read in the parable quoted earlier in this chapter, do as the first servant did initially: fall on your face before God and plead for His mercy. Receive God's forgiveness for your life, not just for an isolated deed.

God's Word promises us, *"If we confess our sins, He is faithful and just to forgive us our sins and to cleanse us from all unrighteousness"* (1 John 1:9).

Once you have received God's forgiveness, forgive yourself. Let the past be the past. But do so with the words of Jesus ringing in your ear: *"Go and sin no more"* (John 8:11). Make a decision that you are *not* going to continue to sin. Ask God to give you the strength and power not to sin.

The first servant made the mistake of getting God's forgiveness and forgiving himself, but then "forgetting" that he had once been a sinner and had been forgiven. God has placed in us an ability to remember for one reason: so we won't repeat our past sins. In heaven, we won't have this memory because we won't need it. We will be forever freed from all impulses and desires to sin, and we will no longer live in a fallen world. Any remembrance of sin would bring grief and sorrow to our hearts. But, until that day, we live on this earth, and we need to remember that we are sinners set free from our sin by the shed blood of Jesus Christ.

Time and again, the people of the Old Testament were called to days of "remembrance" regarding their past sins and God's deliverance and forgiveness of them. We need to remind ourselves often that we are "sinners saved by grace." Moving on in your life, forgiving yourself, shedding the burden of sin's guilt and shame, walking forward in the power of the Holy Spirit—all of that is God's will for you. But it is also His will that you remember that you have sinned and been forgiven, for it is that remembrance that creates in you a merciful and compassionate heart toward others.

Confront with Compassion

It is only after you have confessed and been forgiven of your sin, and only after you have forgiven yourself but have not forgotten God's forgiveness, that you should confront your spouse about the way he or she is trespassing against you.

Never go to your spouse to confront your spouse about his or her sin or "trespasses" against you with anger or emotions that are out of control. Your spouse will not be able to hear what you have to say if your words are flooded with tears, are spoken in a voice that is too loud, or are laced with vulgar language. Ask God to give you a calm heart and a clear mind as you go into a settling of accounts with your spouse.

And, above all, confront with your heart filled with compassion. Be aware that the person who is "sinning" against you may not even know he is sinning, or he may be trying desperately to justify his sin. State the "account" clearly, just as Jesus indicated in His parable. Deal with *facts*. You can state the fact about how you feel, saying, "I feel hurt," or "I feel anger," but don't say, "You hurt me," or "You made me angry." Accept your feelings as being *your* feelings. Accept your perception of the situation as being your perception. Recognize that this is the accounting *you* have. If there's error in the way you have done your accounting, open yourself up to the possibility that you may need to adjust your accounts.

Most of the small stuff is obvious and real and concrete. Being thirty minutes late is thirty minutes. A room filled with old take-out food containers and newspapers is a room filled with old take-out food containers and newspapers. Cite real examples, real situations, real words spoken, and real incidents.

Stay focused not only on what is obvious and objectively observable, but also on what is immediate and isolated in time. Don't use words like *always* or *never:* "You never do this for me," "You always say this," "You never have...," "You always will...." Keep focused on the current "account" before you. Don't bring up past accounts that were paid or forgiven. Stay current. Say, "In this one instance, you...," or "I want to talk to you about this one time when...."

Ask the person to acknowledge the reality of the situation. Your spouse may not think you have a right to be hurt or angry, but that's not the first step. The first step is to make sure you are both talking about the same situation, tightly defined and narrowly focused.

Once you have agreement on the "account" that is at issue, deal with what can or should be done. The truth is, you have feelings and an emotional response to life, and so does your spouse. What hurts you, hurts you. What angers your spouse, angers your spouse. Whether you believe that the hurt or anger is justified or not, face up to the fact that your *spouse's* feelings are real; they are valid to your spouse, and they are part of the equation that has to be dealt with. Seek a common ground of understanding.

Give your spouse an opportunity to admit his or her fault and to apologize. If you are the spouse being confronted, be quick to admit your fault and to apologize. Now, an apology that is "too quick" can be a false apology; it can be an apology just to get out of the uncomfortable confrontation. Be sincere in making an apology. If you aren't, you are chalking up just one more thing about which you will need to apologize down the line!

Don't necessarily press your spouse for an apology in that moment of confrontation. Your spouse may not be able to react that quickly. You may need to say, "I hope you will think about what I have said. If we can't reach resolution on this right now, perhaps we need to discuss it more after you've had a chance to think about it."

Then remember to discuss it again. Your bringing up the issue once doesn't mean you've resolved the issue. The issue is not resolved until forgiveness is voiced and received.

Even if you can't reach resolution and forgiveness as part of that initial encounter of confrontation, state your love for your spouse. State that you believe in your marriage, you are committed to your marriage, you believe for the highest and best for your spouse, and you know in your heart that God is working in both of you to heal you and to bring you to the character likeness of Jesus. State your willingness to forgive and grow and change, but also state your desire to see your spouse be willing to own up to the trespass, seek forgiveness, grow, and change.

Come to the Moment of Forgiveness

Discuss what you need to discuss about a difference between you until you come to the moment of forgiveness. *Mutually* forgive each other. Forgive each other for causing pain or heartache or frustration or concern. Forgive each other for what has been done or said. Forgive each other for misunderstanding what was done or said. Forgive each other for a lack of sensitivity or for having too much unwarranted sensitivity. Come to the point where you agree that a wrong has been committed and where you agree to ask and receive forgiveness from each other.

This may not happen in five minutes, or an hour, or a day, or even several days.

In the time between confrontation and forgiveness, be pleasant to your spouse. Don't put up a wall of silence between you. Don't draw a line in the bed, saying, "You stay on your side, and don't let even your big toe cross that line." Don't mistreat your spouse. Don't walk off and not return for a couple of days. If you take any of these approaches, you are only adding to the problem. You are creating more trespassing that needs to be confronted!

Go Forward

There's nothing in this parable of Jesus that indicates either of these servants ceased to be a servant of the master. The master did not "fire" his servant for chalking up a huge debt. In the end, he turned him over to the "torturer" with the intent that he work to pay his debt. If we fail to receive the forgiveness of God and forgive those who sin against us, we also will find ourselves in a torture chamber. We will find ourselves having to "be everything," "do everything," and "accomplish everything" totally on our own strength, ability, and intelligence. And since that is never possible, we will be under the high stress and emotional torture that come with constant striving. People who are forever seeking to earn God's forgiveness are tortured people. They work hard and struggle greatly but never make any progress because God's forgiveness cannot be earned; it can only be received. God allows us to be turned over to the torturer so that we might again plead for forgiveness and give up our self-striving ways.

In the aftermath of conflict, you are still married.

The main point, however, is that these servants did not leave the service of their master. The same is true for your marriage.

In the aftermath of conflict, you are still married. Work to make the changes that need to be made to avoid future sinning or trespassing. Choose to grow in your relationship with Christ Jesus. Choose to read the Word with even greater desire to apply it to your marriage. Choose to do what you know God's Word is calling you to do. Make positive changes that result in positive growth.

Then, and only then, can you look back on that confrontation and say, "It was for good. God used that to change us, build us up, and make us more useful for His purposes."

Don't allow sin and confrontation to tear you down or pull you apart. Rather, see the confronting of sin as a means of your coming closer together and growing together and being prepared together for even greater ministry to others and usefulness in the kingdom of God.

Forgiveness can save and transform a marriage.

Freely you have received forgiveness from God; freely give it.

12

Defuse Your Anger

Marriage Commandment #9:
Thou Shalt Not Go to Bed Angry

✣

*Do not let the sun go down on your wrath, nor give
place to the devil.*
—Ephesians 4:26–27

The Bible teaches about anger: *"Be angry, and do not sin"*
(Ephesians 4:26). What great balance in that one statement!

Anger itself is not a sin. Anger is a God-given emotion. One
of the benefits of anger is that it motivates us to make changes in
our lives and to do something about the injustices we see around
us. The plan of God, however, is that we channel our anger into
positive behavior—we make changes, we establish new habits, we
seek justice, and we reach out to help those who are in need. We
must never let our anger turn into sin—erupt into hateful words,
lash out in abusive language or actions, or cause us to lose control
of our tempers and hit things or hit people.

All of us have to deal with anger from time to time because we
all find ourselves in situations that are antagonistic. We find someone challenging, threatening, or offending us or those we love. In
some cases, we encounter people intent on hurting or harming us
or those we love. Anger is the normal response.

A number of words in the Bible are "variations" on the anger theme. They include *contention* or *contentious, wrath, vengeance,* and *indignation.* Each of these has its place. We should feel anger at our own sin. We should feel anger when we are the victims of others' sin. But, again, there's no place in God's Word for misusing anger.

There's no place in God's Word for misusing anger.

An eruption of anger in a marriage is very often the result of conflict or a manifestation of conflict, but it is more than that. Anger fuels conflict. It takes a small conflict and magnifies it.

Confront your anger. God's Word says,

> *The discretion of a man makes him slow to anger, and his glory is to overlook a transgression.*　　(Proverbs 19:11)

Some things need to be ignored. Some small nuisances and differences in a marriage simply need to be overlooked. They need to be let go—never to take root, never to be dwelled upon, never to be stored up for later retaliation.

"But I was born with a hot temper," you may say. My response is this: "Then grow up and grow out of that hot temper." It's not God's will for you to have a hot temper and to sin as a result of that hot temper getting out of control.

It Really Does Take Two to Fight

The old saying, "It takes two to tango," is true. If you don't choose to respond to anger with anger, you will be well on your way to resolving the conflict that is underlying an angry outburst. The Bible says, *"A soft answer turns away wrath, but a harsh word stirs up anger"* (Proverbs 15:1).

Choose *not* to fight back.

Now, does this mean that you should hold in all your feelings and store them up so you can erupt at a later time? Does it mean that you should give your spouse the "silent treatment," staring at your spouse as if he or she is totally worthless or utterly ridiculous? No. The proper response is to speak back truth to your spouse with a *"soft answer."* A soft answer is just that—an answer that is low in volume, soft in tone, without cynicism or sarcasm, and reasonable. A soft answer is an answer that says, "I can tell that you are upset. Let's talk about this in a way in which I can understand all that you are trying to say to me."

A soft answer is not a sermon. It is not a holier-than-thou put-down. A soft answer is not a pronouncement of "You're stupid" or "You're ridiculous"—not even if you whisper that response! A soft answer is one that the angry spouse perceives to be "soft." It's one that "goes down" well. It's an answer that softens the harshness of the person's anger. It's an answer that brings cool calm to the overheated passions of the moment.

The softest answer of all is the one that says, "I love you so much. I'm sorry. Please forgive me." There is nothing better to cool down a heated argument.

The fact is, if you speak out of your own anger, you are likely to say things you don't mean or that you will regret later. The Bible says, *"A wise man fears and departs from evil, but a fool rages and is self-confident. A quick-tempered man acts foolishly"* (Proverbs 14:16–17). Don't get sucked into foolish words or foolish deeds. Don't rage at the wind. Ask God to give you calm in your spirit so you can see the situation more objectively, and then respond out of reason and the truth of God's Word.

Deal with Your Temper

If you are the one in the marriage who tends to erupt with anger, ask God to help you and to change you. Speak to yourself, "I don't have to do that! I don't have to respond that way! My negative emotions don't have to dictate how I am. I am a child of God. I can act and speak in calm strength. I do not need to speak in anger."

If you feel anger rising up in you, simply walk away. Get control of yourself. The old saying, "Count to ten before you speak," is a good one; but in some cases you may need to increase the number. Count to fifty if necessary!

Even better than counting is this: recite some Scriptures to yourself. Remind yourself of who you are in the Lord. See yourself as a loving, peaceful, joyful person because of what God has done for you through Jesus Christ His Son. See yourself as a person who has been given God's Holy Spirit for guidance and direction. Speak to yourself as a person who is growing in kindness, goodness, mercy, patience, and self-control because these are the traits that the Holy Spirit desires to manifest in your life.

Dont Allow Buildup ➤

Part of the reason some people explode in anger is that they allow small problems to build up over time without addressing those small problems when they are small. They say, "Oh, it's not worth it. Why make a fuss over something so little?"

If that "something" is irritating you to the point that you remember it and continue to hold it against your spouse, that "something" is not small. Address the issue in a soft tone, saying, "I'd appreciate it if...," or "I know this is a small thing, but I find it very irritating when you.... I know you don't want to irritate me. I'm going to try not to be irritated, but would you also try not to...?"

Don't Lump Problems Together

Another habit that tends to cause explosions of anger is the habit of lumping problems together so that no one problem can be isolated or addressed. Rather, the small negative feelings about a host of small problems are put together to create one giant negative feeling about a mountain of problems! The words we tend to shout are *always, never, should,* and *or else.* We give ultimatums and threaten severe, vengeful consequences.

Stop! Take one problem at a time. Stay in the present.

Get to the Core Problem

Recognize that expressions of anger in your marriage are indicative of a problem in the angry spouse. The core of that problem might be unhappiness. It might be a failure in the person's ability to express himself—a lack of knowing how to say and act in a way that is positive. The core problem may be an emotional illness or an emotional instability. It may be a physical illness or a chemical imbalance. The problem may be an addiction.

Before you can help an angry spouse find healing, you need to know the core cause of the anger. Do your best to determine *why* your spouse is angry. If your spouse doesn't know the cause of his or her own anger, get professional help.

A Manifestation of Opposition

The opposite of cooperation is opposition. Opposition is very often marked by a manifestation of anger.

The person who doesn't want to cooperate in a marriage is a person who is likely to fly off the handle at the least little problem, say hurtful and hateful things, and even resort to abuse. The problem is not in the person who is the recipient of this anger or abuse. The problem is in the spouse who has something going on deep inside that erupts in anger, pride, and feelings of "opposition" against anyone or anything that confronts, challenges, or questions his or her worthiness and esteem *in his or her opinion.*

The angry, prideful, abusive person who erupts in verbal or physical abuse is a person with deep inner problems. Most abused spouses feel that they must have done something to provoke the abuse. That is very often *not* the case. The abusive person has a seething anger deep within that is just looking for an excuse to be vented. That deep inner anger may be related to something in the past. It may be related to the person's feelings of low self-value or low self-worth. It may be related to the fact that the person was a victim of abuse as a child. There are numerous reasons that only the person can isolate and that only God can heal. The abusive person needs divine healing—a genuine healing of the soul—before he or she can relate in a normal way to other people.

Until that day comes, a person with deep anger is more likely to be opposed to a spouse than to be in cooperation with a spouse. The person desperately wants and needs to be loved, forgiven, understood, and built up, but the fact is, he has these deep, desperate needs because he doesn't love, forgive, or understand himself, and he hasn't fully received the love, forgiveness, and understanding that God offers to him.

You as a spouse cannot do for an angry, abusive, opposing spouse what that spouse will not do for him- or herself. You can love that person, pray for that person, and do your best to build up that person emotionally, but in the end, only God can truly heal that person. Pray for your spouse's healing. Encourage the person to get wise advice from a godly counselor. And protect yourself and your children against violence.

Never Hit Your Spouse

One of the greatest shocks I received in doing marriage counseling was the realization that a significant number of married people hit each other. They don't just shout at each other in anger—they actually punch, slap, kick, and pummel each other. One man told me that his wife had kicked him black and blue to the point he couldn't sit down without feeling pain.

> If you get angry and you don't know what to do with your hands, sit on them.

If you are hitting your spouse, stop it. That includes punching your spouse in the arm or slapping your spouse across the mouth. It includes hitting your spouse on the behind or "spanking" your spouse. The same goes for shoving or pushing your spouse. If you get angry and you don't know what to do with your hands, sit on them.

If you are being hit by your spouse, put an end to allowing that to happen. Leave the house. Walk away. Let your spouse know that you will *not* be the victim of physical abuse.

The Bible says, *"Make no friendship with an angry man, and with a furious man do not go, lest you learn his ways and set a snare for your soul"* (Proverbs 22:24–25). Don't get in a car with an angry spouse, especially if that spouse is behind the wheel!

The Aftermath of Remorse

Often when a person erupts in anger, he or she feels deep remorse or regret afterward. Unfortunately, the damage has been done. If you have erupted in anger, realize that you have very likely wounded your spouse. Don't be too quick to say, "I'm sorry"—that will sound insincere—but do apologize to your spouse for losing your temper.

Do apologize for words that you wish you had never said.

Ask your spouse to forgive you.

Having a remorseful attitude is never a satisfactory substitute for a genuine change of behavior. I once heard the story of a little girl whose brother would hit her and then immediately say, "I'm sorry, I'm sorry." She said, "Listen here, buster. *Sorry* doesn't mean a thing! You're going to *be* sorry if you have to say 'I'm sorry' one more time!" The fact is, if you are truly sorry for your angry outburst, you will seek to control your anger.

A Positive Direction for Anger

Rather than turn your anger toward your spouse, turn your anger toward the devil. He's the real enemy. He's the one who is trying to destroy the peace between you and your spouse. One woman said to me, "I get mad when I see that the enemy has come into my home and is trying to take authority over it. I get mad at how the devil tries to keep me from walking in the inheritance God has promised me. In my anger, I let him know what's what. I sometimes shout, 'Jesus, rebuke the devil out of here right now. Devil, you have to go!'"

Turn your anger into intercession. Turn your anger into songs of praise. Turn your anger into the voicing aloud of God's Word. When you do so, you are not only venting your anger in a positive way, but you are actually bringing healing to your own spirit.

Keep in mind that a display of anger damages your testimony. It keeps you from expressing what you believe about the Lord.

Anger also brings the judgment of God back on you. Jesus said, *"Whoever is angry with his brother without a cause shall be in danger of the judgment"* (Matthew 5:22). Why? Because anger is at the root of all violence, war, murder, and willful destructive behavior that maims, hurts, injures, and destroys. Sinful behavior always brings the judgment of God.

Ultimately, you have a decision: allow the devil to provoke you to rage or allow the Spirit of Christ to be greater in you than the spirit of the enemy. Choose how you will behave. It's not an automatic thing. Your behavior is subject to your will, and, therefore, it is subject to your *choosing*.

Anger may have become a habit for you. If that's the case, then choose to develop a new habit.

Yelling and screaming may have become your automatic response for dealing with something that you find troublesome or problematic. If that's the case, then choose to develop new communication skills.

Confront Yourself First

If you are angry, you will eventually vent your anger. The result is going to be a confrontation of some sort. Choose to confront yourself *first*. Have a talk with yourself about the problem that is irritating you. Then have a talk with God about the situation. Ask God to reveal to you how you can avoid the problematic situation that resulted in your anger. Ask God to heal that area of weakness or emotional turmoil inside you so that you won't live constantly with anger just under the surface. Say to the Lord, "God, before I can deal with anybody else, You have to deal with me. Help me to deal with the real issues in me first."

Don't point your finger at anybody else until you have first pointed your finger at yourself.

Don't point your finger at anybody else until you have first pointed your finger at yourself.

Then, and only then, go to the person who may have been involved in the situation that caused you to feel anger, and express your opinion, your idea, your solution, your feelings, your response. If you go in the wrong spirit, you will only provoke anger in that person, and then you both will be operating in anger. Before you know it, you can have a blowout situation. Go to the privacy of your bathroom, your car, or a private area of your home or workplace and pray, "God, give me grace. Don't allow this anger in me to escalate out of control. Show me what it is that you want me to say and do. Show me how Jesus would react and respond in this situation."

Confront Privately

Jesus taught, *"If your brother sins against you, go and tell him his fault between you and him alone"* (Matthew 18:15). You don't need to broadcast to the world, to your friends, to your mother or your auntie, or to your children all that your spouse is doing to trespass against you. Go to your spouse alone. A confrontation should not be a public confrontation, but a very private confrontation. Don't raise your voice so that the neighbors can hear every word through the walls of your apartment. Don't talk about your grievances in the presence of your children.

Do go. Jesus said, *"Tell him his fault."*

However, do keep your confrontation between the two of you. Keep it private. What is solved privately is truly resolved. There's nobody else to whom you must then go and ask forgiveness for dragging them into the fray.

Taking Charge of What Causes Anger

The management of anger is an issue of self-control.

The Bible teaches that the control of anger is within our ability, our will. We read in Proverbs 16:32, *"He who is slow to anger is better than the mighty, and he who rules his spirit than he who takes a city."* Dealing with your anger is a matter of governing your own life. To deal with anger is a mark of leadership, of maturity, and of emotional health.

Ask God to help you control your anger.

Less Sensitivity May Be Required

The Lord may very well ask you to deal with your own sensitivity. Sometimes we are just too sensitive as human beings. We are too quick to feel slighted, hurt, or rejected.

Early in my marriage, I often misread what my wife was doing or saying. There were times when she seemed way too emotional. I went to God and asked for wisdom, and the Lord revealed to me, "This isn't something in her mind or spirit. She's responding out of the hormone changes in her body." I came to realize that there were certain times of the month in which my wife was going to be quicker to cry or express anger than other times...and it had nothing to do with me. It had to do with what was going on chemically in her body. I needed to be less sensitive in how I "took" some of the things she might say or do.

Better Communication May Be Warranted

Sometimes we have a misunderstanding in the words we use. The definition of a word in your spouse's mind might be very different from the definition you have for that word. Get some understanding flowing between you so that you know what you are talking about! A woman once shared with me that when she was in her twenties, she shared an apartment with a woman from France. This roommate also spoke German, and English was actually her third language. The roommate's boyfriend was from the Middle East. He spoke Armenian as his first language, Arabic as his second language, and English as his third language. The roommate didn't speak a word of Armenian or Arabic, and the Armenian boyfriend didn't speak a word of French or German. She said, "You can only begin to imagine the communication problems that occurred."

Sometimes it may feel as if you and your spouse are speaking two different languages. You may be! Before you erupt in anger, ask for a translation or a definition. You may have no cause for anger after all.

Do your best to defuse the situations or circumstances that seem to give rise to anger. Deal with the trigger points and "hot buttons" in your relationship.

As you do, you will find it much easier to prevent conflicts. And, especially in the case of anger, prevention is always the best cure!

13

Pray with Expectation

Marriage Commandment #10:
Thou Shalt Pray for Each Other

❖❖❖

Rejoice always, pray without ceasing, in everything give thanks.
—1 Thessalonians 5:16–18

I am amazed at how many people come to a marriage counseling session and admit they have never prayed for their spouse. In fact, they seem surprised at the question. They've never even thought about praying for their spouse.

There are at least two reasons you should pray for your spouse.

First, if your spouse is not a believer, you should pray for your spouse to accept Jesus Christ as his or her Savior. That's the number-one prayer you need to be praying. God won't overstep the free will He gave to all mankind and change your spouse apart from your spouse's will. He won't "zap" your spouse in some way to make your spouse shape up, fly right, or see things your way. Pray diligently for your spouse's salvation, and don't give up on that prayer. You may be the only person who is praying for your spouse to come to the Lord.

Second, if your spouse is a believer, you should pray for your spouse just as you pray for all other believers. The Bible has some wonderful prayers for believers. Read what the apostle Paul and his associate Timothy prayed for the Colossians. Paul opened his letter to the Colossians by saying, *"We give thanks to the God and Father of our Lord Jesus Christ, praying always for you"* (Colossians 1:3). Then a little later in that first part of his letter we read what they prayed:

> [We] *do not cease to pray for you, and to ask that you may be filled with the knowledge of His will in all wisdom and spiritual understanding; that you may walk worthy of the Lord, fully pleasing Him, being fruitful in every good work and increasing in the knowledge of God; strengthened with all might, according to His glorious power, for all patience and longsuffering with joy; giving thanks to the Father who has qualified us to be partakers of the inheritance of the saints in the light. He has delivered us from the power of darkness and conveyed us into the kingdom of the Son of His love, in whom we have redemption through His blood, the forgiveness of sins.* (vv. 9–14)

Take a look at several key things Paul and Timothy prayed for these saints. These are things you can and should be praying for your spouse who is a fellow believer.

"We give thanks." Have you thanked the Lord today for your spouse? Have you thanked the Lord for your marriage? Have you thanked the Lord for creating your spouse, for bringing your spouse to you, for giving you to your spouse in marriage, for the many ways in which your spouse is a blessing to your life—not only in the past, but also in the present? Are you thanking and praising God for the things you believe are in keeping with His Word, and that you therefore can anticipate as being things for which you will be thankful in the future?

"Do not cease to pray." Have you given up on your spouse? If so, ask God to rekindle your desire to pray for your spouse and to do so with faith, trusting God to hear your prayers and answer them according to His timing, His methods, and His purposes. Do you pray for your spouse once in a while or just when you have conflict? Or are you praying for your spouse every day, several times a day?

"Filled with the knowledge of His will." Pray that God will cause your spouse to have a deep hunger to know the Bible and to want to know and do God's will. Pray for your spouse to be *filled* with the knowledge of God—a knowledge of not only the Bible but also the Lord's presence. Pray that your spouse will be able to hear the Holy Spirit speaking in his or her heart.

Pray that the Lord will give your spouse understanding about how to be a good spouse, how to treat you in your marriage, how to deal with your children, and how to relate to other members of your extended families.

Pray that the Lord will give you an understanding about the purpose that God has for your family in the world today. What is it that God desires you and your spouse to accomplish together in His kingdom? What are you called to give of your time, energy, talents, and resources to win souls and to influence people to grow in Christ? Pray for an understanding of God's will!

"Filled with…all wisdom and spiritual understanding." Pray that God will show your spouse what to do, how to do it, when to do it, where to go, what to say, and how to act. Most of all, pray that your spouse will have an understanding about why God created him or her. Pray that your spouse will have a growing understanding about who he or she is in the Lord and what he or she has been created to be and to do on this earth. Pray that your spouse will have a growing understanding regarding his or her spiritual gifts, natural talents, and the ministry that God has planned for your spouse's life.

Not everybody is called to full-time Christian work, but every Christian is called to be a witness for the Lord Jesus every day of his or her life, in all situations, and in the presence of every person he or she encounters. To be an effective witness takes wisdom and spiritual understanding. It takes an ability to discern good from evil, to discern the work of demons and the work of angels, to see what the Holy Spirit is doing and to understand what the devil is up to.

"Walk worthy of the Lord, fully pleasing Him." Pray that your spouse will exhibit godly character wherever he or she goes. Pray

that others will see Christ in your spouse. Pray that your spouse will not get involved in things that are sinful or in things that

Pray that others will see Christ in your spouse.

are a waste of time and money. Pray that your spouse will have his or her priorities in line with God's Word and God's will—and that your spouse will spend his or her time and talent doing things that bring glory to His name.

"Being fruitful in every good work." Pray that your spouse will be diligent in working and that his or her work will be rewarded with good fruit. Pray that your spouse will do work that is worthy of promotion, increase, a raise, recognition, and appreciation. Pray that all benefits—both material and spiritual—will accrue to your spouse's life. Pray that your spouse will enjoy the fulfillment and satisfaction that comes when you know that you have done your best, that God is pleased, and that God will use what you have done to further His purposes on this earth. Pray that your spouse's words and deeds will not return void, but like bread upon the water, will cause an increase in the kingdom of God—an increase in souls won to Christ, an increase in people influenced to do good, and an increase in joy, peace, faith, truth, and love.

"Increasing in the knowledge of God." This knowledge isn't merely a knowledge of what the Bible says. It is a knowledge of the Lord Himself that comes through times of prayer and meditation and in sitting quietly before the Lord listening to what He might speak to your heart. Pray that your spouse will have quiet moments with God, and that your spouse will be challenged to pray more, to listen more, to reflect more on the things that are truly eternal and, therefore, vitally important.

"Strengthened with all might." Very specifically, pray that your spouse will have enduring might—the patience and long-suffering necessary to stick with a task and to be faithful to a relationship, including your marriage—every day of his or her life. Pray that this "enduring" in faithfulness will not be a burden but a joy to your spouse. Pray that God will give your spouse a "want to" spirit to go along with His "have to" commandments.

"Partakers of the inheritance of the saints." Pray that your spouse will walk in a way that stores up heavenly reward. Pray

that your spouse will live in such a way that everybody who sees your spouse's life will know that he or she has been saved and transformed by the Lord Jesus Christ.

"Delivered...from the power of darkness." Pray that your spouse will be freed from the temptations, impulses, and desires that lead to sin. Pray that the Lord will deliver your spouse from the attacks of the enemy and that your spouse will live free of oppression, depression, negative impressions, addiction, and suppression. Pray that the devil departs **You will never run out of things to pray for your spouse!** from your spouse and that God sends His holy angels to build a hedge of protection around your spouse, so that your spouse can walk freely and boldly in the power of the Holy Spirit, bringing glory to God's name.

And when you are finished praying all that, if you haven't run out of daylight hours, there are countless other Scriptures that you can pray into your spouse's life. Philemon 4–6 says,

> *I thank my God, making mention of you always in my prayers, hearing of your love and faith which you have toward the Lord Jesus and toward all the saints, that the sharing of your faith may become effective by the acknowledgment of every good thing which is in you in Christ Jesus.*

What a wonderful prayer to pray for your spouse!

Pray for Every *Good* Thing

Find God's promises to you in His Word, and pray those blessings into your spouse's life.

Find God's commandments, and pray that your spouse will be faithful in keeping them.

Read about the miracles. Pray that God will give your spouse the miracles he or she needs.

Trust me on this—you will *never* run out of things to pray for your spouse!

The More You Pray...

A wonderful thing happens as you pray for your spouse. Your heart is opened up toward your spouse, and you have an increasing desire to pray for your spouse and to see your spouse experience all the blessings God desires to give to your spouse and through your spouse to you.

The more you pray for your spouse, the more God will increase the measure of love you have for your spouse.

The more you pray for your spouse, the more you will see your spouse as God sees your spouse.

The more you pray for your spouse, the more your heart will be softened toward your spouse, and the easier it will be for you to forgive your spouse.

Praying with Your Spouse

As much as I am amazed at the number of married folk who don't pray for their spouses, I am also amazed at the number of Christian couples who don't routinely pray together—and as part of their prayer time together, pray for themselves and their marriage.

Jesus said,

> Whatever you bind on earth will be bound in heaven, and whatever you loose on earth will be loosed in heaven. Again I say to you that if two of you agree on earth concerning anything that they ask, it will be done for them by My Father in heaven. For where two or three are gathered together in My name, I am there in the midst of them.
>
> (Matthew 18:18–20)

Two of you gathered in His name? You and your spouse qualify! Jesus said that *whatever* you agree about in His name, it would be done.

Now, there are some things that are outside His name. God is not going to hear and honor your prayer to bless your gambling bet at the racetrack. God is not going to hear and honor your prayer to destroy the life of somebody you don't like. God isn't going to hear and honor your prayer to win the Publisher's Clearing House Sweepstakes (which is a form of gambling with odds of a million to one). No, God is going to hear and honor your prayers of agreement that are in keeping with His will and His Word.

What are some of those things?

They are the things that ultimately matter most to you as a married couple and as parents.

God desires that you have a ministry together and a witness to the world about Jesus Christ, your Savior and Lord. Pray for that ministry. Pray that God will "loose" it in your hearts and minds, and then pray that God will give you the guidance and courage to "loose" it into your neighborhood, your community, and the world.

God desires for you to have your needs met. Pray that all forms of sickness, discouragement, and oppression will be "bound" so that you can "loose" all the creativity, energy, and skills God has built into you. Pray that God will "loose" opportunities on your behalf. Pray that God will "loose" the money you need, the provision you must have to accomplish the work He has called you to do. Pray that God will give you health, strength, wisdom, knowledge, energy, and motivation. All those things are promised to you in His Word. All those things are in line with the way heaven operates and the way God intends for His kingdom on this earth to function!

God desires the enemy to be banished from your life. Pray that God will build up your resistance to temptation and give you a hearty hatred for evil. Pray that God will give you a greater desire to pray and to engage in spiritual warfare, in order that your marriage, your children, and your church will be "loosed" from the enemy's clutches and that all the blessings of heaven will be released to you.

Pray that the spiritual gifts God has given you will find full expression—both individually and as a couple.

Pray that God will strengthen your love for each other.

Pray that God will give you increased compassion, not only for each other and for your children, but also for those you encounter in the course of your work, your recreation, and your worship.

Pray specifically for today's needs—the money you need, the decisions you face, the problems you have encountered, the struggles you are enduring, the work that you must do, the people with whom you have scheduled appointments, and the people you will meet randomly in the course of your day.

Pray for the needs that others have brought to you as a couple. Pray for the needs in your church. Pray for those in authority over you, including your pastors and others who teach you and counsel you in the body of Christ. Pray for the lost souls you know and whom God has placed on your heart.

You will never run out of things to pray *together.* And as is true for your personal prayer life, the more you pray together as a couple, the more you will see God at work. **If you want Jesus to be in your marriage, pray together.** Encourage each other to praise and thank God for the answers He gives. Encourage each other to see the many ways in which God is blessing you and causing you to defeat the devil and walk in victory. The more you do this, the more you will want to do this as a couple.

Don't just become a person of prayer. Become a marriage of prayer! Your power of agreement will be fruitful in binding the enemy and in releasing the power of God. And as Jesus Himself promised, He will be there in the midst of your prayer together. If you want Jesus to be in your marriage, pray together. He's right there with you as you pray!

14

Resolving Conflict in the Bedroom

❖❖❖

Afellow pastor recently shared with me a marriage counseling experience he had. He said, "These two people have been married for thirty-three years. But they haven't had sex for more than twenty years."

"What happened?" I asked.

"According to the wife, her husband was always angry, and his anger got her so upset she didn't feel like having sex. He went along with that for a while, and eventually it got to be a pattern. The trouble is, he then had an affair. The wife was obviously even more upset at that and used it as an excuse to never have sex with him again. He still loved his wife, and she was willing to have him around to pay the bills and be a father to the children, so they have just lived together that way."

"Why did she come to you?"

"Well, it seems the husband gave up his mistress years ago, but then he turned to the mistress of alcohol. The wife came to me saying, 'Pastor, my husband has a drinking problem, and he's been unfaithful. What do you think I should do about him?'"

"What did you say?"

"I said, 'Ma'am, just why do you think your husband had an affair and now has a drinking problem?' She said, 'He just doesn't have any self-control.' I said, 'No, ma'am, that isn't the reason. *You* are the reason. If you want to fix this relationship, fix your attitude and forgive your husband. Then fix your hair, fix your makeup, buy yourself a new sexy nightgown, fix the house with candles and soft music, and take your husband into your bed. *You* can fix this problem."

I couldn't have said it better myself.

Sexually frustrated people are not nice people. It's hard to stay nice if you are fighting a sexual drive. You need to set yourselves a goal in your marriage: "If we have problems regarding our sex life, we are going to deal with them. We're going to address the problems, find answers and solutions, and then act on those answers and solutions."

What God Says about Sexual Intimacy

For us to understand how to resolve conflicts that are primarily sexual, we need to revisit what God says about sexual intimacy. One of the most important passages of Scripture regarding the intimate relationship between a husband and wife is found in 1 Corinthians 7:1–9:

Now concerning the things of which you wrote to me: It is good for a man not to touch a woman. Nevertheless, because of sexual immorality, let each man have his own wife, and let each woman have her own husband. Let the husband render to his wife the affection due her, and likewise also the wife to her husband. The wife does not have authority over her own body, but the husband does. And likewise the husband does not have authority over his own body, but the wife does. Do not deprive one another except with consent for a time, that you may give yourselves to fasting and prayer; and come together again so that Satan does not tempt you because of your lack of self-control. But I say this as a concession, not as a commandment. For I wish that all men were even as I myself. But each one has his own gift from God, one in this manner and another in that. But I say to the unmarried and to the widows: It is good for them if they remain even as I am; but if they cannot exercise self-control, let them marry. For it is better to marry than to burn with passion.

This passage contains three main principles that are important foundations for sexual intimacy in marriage.

Principle #1: Sex Belongs in Marriage

God created the sexual drive in men and women. It is part of His plan to ensure that the human race continues; people need to have sex to make babies so future generations can live. God also made the sexual act an act that gives pleasure, release, and fulfillment to men and women. If sex wasn't pleasurable, people probably wouldn't have sex, and the result would be no babies!

The first purpose of sexual intimacy is fruitfulness. The second purpose of sexual intimacy is pleasure. We tend to have that backward in our world today; we tend to emphasize the pleasure of sex rather than the fruitfulness.

> The first purpose of sexual intimacy is fruitfulness.

Let me add this—if you have any question about specific behaviors, put that behavior to the "fruitfulness test." Ask yourself, "Is what I want to do an act that has the potential for bearing fruit?" If a sexual act doesn't have the potential for producing fruit, don't do it. You'll be making "pleasure" more important than "fruitfulness," and that's a bad precedent to set. It's too easy to transfer that order to other areas of life so that you do things that "feel good" but aren't productive or fruitful. God intended for fruitfulness to be fun, but there's nothing in God's Word that says fun is always fruitful. Get your priorities right when it comes to your sexual behavior, and a lot of other priorities will fall into place for you.

What we know about the way God created us as sexual beings, therefore, is this:

• Sex is supposed to happen between a husband and wife.

• Sex is supposed to be fun.

• Sex is supposed to be kept totally and completely within the bonds of marriage.

Sex Is Limited to Marriage

The reason sex is to be limited to marriage is threefold.

First, sex binds two people together as one flesh. This is a physical reality. Two people who are having sexual intercourse are "one" in their flesh. It's against God's principles for you to be "one" in the flesh with one person one night, with another person the next night, and so on. Sexual union is an act that belongs to marriage alone.

Sex before marriage is wrong. Sex with anybody other than your spouse is wrong.

Second, sex belongs exclusively to marriage because when children are born to that marriage union, children need a father and a mother. They need to be brought up with two parents. That's God's ideal. We've messed it up greatly in our culture and in our nation, but God's ideal is the ideal we Christians still need to pursue with all our hearts, minds, and strength. Sex produces babies, and babies need a stable home with both a father and a mother.

What a husband and wife produce together, they need to raise together.

Third, sex does not begin with that physical act of sexual intercourse. Sex begins in the mind. The "idea" of sex is the first act of foreplay.

Show me two people who are thinking all day about having sex with their spouse, and I'll show you two people who are ready, willing, and eager to have sex the minute they get behind their bedroom door at night! On the other hand, show me two people who are bickering, fighting, and thinking about anything but sex all day, and I'll show you two people who may *have* sex when they are alone, but that sexual union isn't going to be nearly as satisfying or enjoyable to them.

> What a husband and wife produce together, they need to raise together.

The Bible says that your fantasies about sex and your "thoughts" about sex should be fantasies and thoughts involving your spouse.

Otherwise, you are thinking one thing and living out another thing. You are living a "divided life" between what you think about and what you do. You are living a lie, and those who live a lie in this area are going to be people who live a lie in other areas of their lives. They are going to find it easy to be hypocritical or untrustworthy because they are accustomed to thinking one thing and doing another.

Let me also add this—thinking about sex is powerful foreplay. Thoughts arouse passion. If a wife indicates to her husband or promises her husband that they are going to have sex at a certain time, she needs to remember what she has indicated or promised! Don't promise your spouse something you aren't willing to remember and deliver!

Sex Is Intended to Be a Good Part of Marriage

Sex within marriage is normal and pure and good. There's nothing dirty or impure about it. There's no sin associated with it. Sex between a husband and wife was God's idea. After God created woman from man's side, we read these words of the Lord: *"Therefore a man shall leave his father and mother and be joined to his wife, and they shall become one flesh. And they were both naked, the man and his wife, and were not ashamed"* (Genesis 2:24–25). There was nothing unclean, impure, unnatural, immoral, or sinful about their relationship. Adam and Eve enjoyed each other sexually in total innocence and purity.

> Sex within marriage is normal and pure and good.

That's God's plan for marriage. Two virgins—male and female—are to come together after their wedding and become "one flesh" and enjoy each other without any shame.

It's when the devil gets into the mix that things get dirty and complicated. It's when the devil introduces sin into the marriage that sex becomes "polluted" in a person's thinking. Only after Adam and Eve sinned did they know that they were naked. They saw themselves as being needy, incomplete, unclothed, and vulnerable. Prior to that, the thought never crossed their minds that they were vulnerable or needy. They lived in satisfaction and wholeness with each other.

If the conflict in your marriage has sexual roots, ask yourself, "What lie have we been listening to from the devil? What has the devil said to us about sex? What has he said to me? What has he said to my spouse?"

If the conflict in your marriage is sexual, there's a lie of the devil lurking behind the scenes. Expose that lie to the truth.

It may have been a lie told to the wife. "Sex is for men. Women aren't supposed to enjoy this. Just put up with it, and maybe he'll eventually change his mind." That's a lie!

It may have been a lie told to the husband. "You don't need to be faithful to your wife. Get your needs met. If your wife doesn't meet your needs, find another woman."

It may have been the lie, "It's okay to have sex before marriage."

It may have been the lie, "Sex is dirty."

If a person has had sexual intercourse with a person other than his or her spouse, another set of lies can come into play, such as, "Your spouse should do what that lover did," or "Your spouse isn't as 'good' in bed." Comparisons are made—many of them unconscious. Because behavior has not been in line with God's Word, attitudes in the wake of that behavior are also not in line with God's Word. A lie can lead to behavior; a lie can also flow out of behavior.

Expose those lies to the truth!

Sex between Married People Is "Undefiled"

The Bible says in Hebrews 13:4, *"Marriage is honorable among all, and the bed undefiled."* God holds marriage to be honorable. *"Undefiled"* means that whatever two married people decide to do sexually with each other—including how often they choose to have sex, where they choose to have sex, and how they choose to have sex—is all permissible and without any form of "uncleanness" attached to it. *"Undefiled"* means it's not wrong, as long as it's kept in the confines of God's Word.

Principle #2: Your Body Is Not Your Own

At the time the apostle Paul was writing to the Corinthians, many Greek women were deprived of both emotional and sexual fulfillment. Their husbands had become so "aesthetic" that they had ceased to have sex with their wives. When these men became Christians, some of them transferred their aesthetic philosophy to their theology. They decided to become so "spiritual" that they ceased to have sex with their wives. Paul said to them, "You're wrong." He wrote,

> Let the husband render to his wife the affection due her, and likewise also the wife to her husband. The wife does not have authority over her own body, but the husband does. And likewise the husband does not have authority over his own body, but the wife does. Do not deprive one another except with consent for a time, that you may give yourselves to fasting and prayer; and come together again so that Satan does not tempt you because of your lack of self-control. (1 Corinthians 7:3–5)

Notice that Paul said that a husband needs to show *affection* to his wife. In too many cases, a husband demands sex from his wife, and she ends up feeling used. Too many husbands have the attitude, "Meet my need," and, as soon as their needs are met, they roll over and go to sleep. Husband, that's not what a wife needs. She needs to be romanced. She needs to be kissed and held and enticed and wooed. She needs to hear you say to her, "I love you." She needs to be caressed. She needs to hear tender words, complimentary words, respectful words, appreciative words.

Part of showing affection to your wife means talking to your wife.

Part of showing affection to your wife means showing respect for her by being clean when you crawl into bed with her. Showing affection means taking a shower and brushing your teeth!

You Have No Right of Refusal

Paul let the Corinthians know that married people have no right of refusal to their spouse when it comes to meeting sexual needs. A wife has no privilege to say to her husband, "I reject you sexually." A husband has no privilege to say to his wife, "I reject you sexually."

Certainly, there are times when a person cannot or should not engage in sexual intercourse because of medical problems. But when those medical problems are resolved, you should return to normal sexual relations.

If there are problems in your ability or desire to participate in sexual intimacy, address those problems! Take a couple of aspirin for that headache. Find out what turns you on. Talk to somebody about your impotency. Address the problem and seek a solution.

Paul also said that there may be times when you agree together that you are going to fast and pray about a particular matter, and part of your fasting is going to be abstinence from sexual intercourse. After that time of fasting and prayer, you are to come together again.

Note that I've said several times that the two of you need to "agree together." That isn't going to happen unless you are willing to talk about sex with each other.

"But I'm too embarrassed," you may say.

Get over it. There should be no room for embarrassment with your spouse.

Your spouse may have a need for sex every day. You may not have that need. You need to reach a compromise.

Your spouse may like some things that you don't like. You need to reach a compromise.

Your spouse may feel rejected any time that you don't give everything he or she wants. You may not even be aware that your spouse is feeling rejected. You need to talk. How else is your spouse going to know how you feel?

If you don't talk with your spouse about your sexual needs, desires, and your sex life as a married couple, you will be easy prey for the tempter. The devil will feed you the lie, "Well, if your spouse won't do this, somebody else will." The devil may feed you the lie, "Well, if this is what marriage is like, maybe you should go back to being unmarried." The devil may whisper the lie, "You have a right to do whatever you want." Expose the lie to the truth. Talk about sex with your spouse.

Talk about Your Expectations and Methods

A great deal of conflict in the bedroom rises from a failure to communicate about expectations and methodology. Two people usually enter marriage expecting to enjoy each other sexually. But they usually come from two different perceptions about *how* sexual intercourse is to be carried out. They may have the same goal of sexual fulfillment, but they have different expectations about how to get to that point of fulfillment. Talk about your expectations.

What do you like? What don't you like? Do you like to be touched or held in a certain way more than in another way? Your spouse can't read your mind. Express your likes and dislikes.

You may say, "Well, I don't know what I like." Do some exploring and experimenting with each other. Talk about how you feel afterward. Don't criticize each other; rather, educate each other.

Keep in mind that we are creatures of habit. Don't get into a sexual routine—continue to experiment and explore each other. Continue to talk. Continue to fantasize about your spouse, and seek to fulfill those fantasies with your spouse.

Principle #3: You May Not Feel a Need to Marry

Paul wrote this to the unmarried and widows in Corinth: *"It is good for them if they remain even as I am; but if they cannot exercise self-control, let them marry. For it is better to marry than to burn with passion"* (1 Corinthians 7:8–9).

If you are unmarried or a widow and you don't have a strong sexual drive, don't feel compelled to marry. Give yourself to the Lord. Trust Him to give you the self-control you need to stay pure.

But if you have a strong sexual drive and God has not called you to be celibate, then you need to find yourself a spouse.

There's no justification, excuse, or license for fornication in God's Word.

Those who *"burn with passion"* are those who don't have a godly outlet for sexual expression. Let me assure you that if you are burning with passion, you'll find it difficult to concentrate on anything other than sex. You'll find all your conversations, thoughts, and feelings moving toward sex; you'll find it difficult to create anything beautiful or productive that doesn't have sexual overtones to it. If you have a "burning passion" for sex, then you *need* to marry. And once you are married, you need to find the full expression for that passion with your spouse. There is no justification, excuse, or license for going outside your marriage vows to put out the fires you feel.

> There's no justification, excuse, or license for fornication in God's Word.

I once had a man say to me, "God made me with a huge sexual appetite. He must have intended for me to have more than one woman because no one woman can possibly satisfy me." My response to him was this: "Ask God to deal with your appetite."

Let me repeat: there is no provision in God's Word for you to get your sexual needs met outside your marriage. Ask God to deal with your sexual appetite, and you will likely find that one woman not only can satisfy you, but does satisfy you.

When You Base Your Sex Life on Godly Principles

Several things happen when you choose to base your sex life on godly principles.

First, you will come to marriage pure—a virgin—and you will not have preconceived notions about what should and shouldn't be the sexual behavior of your spouse. You will not have a lot of emotional "baggage" that you have to unload when it comes to what is and isn't done sexually.

Second, you will see sex as God intended it to be seen: as a means of being fruitful, as a means of giving and receiving pleasure, and as a means of meeting a need in another person.

The person who comes to marriage with a right understanding of sex will no longer be solely intent on getting his or her needs met. Rather, that person will have the attitude, "How can I meet the need of my spouse, given the fact that I am the only person who is authorized to meet this need in my spouse's life?"

Let me tell you, that is a huge shift in focus from the way most people think about sex. Most people come to a sexual relationship with the attitude, "What can this person do for me? How good can this person make me feel?" The godly spouse has the attitude, "What can I do for my spouse? How good can I make my spouse feel?"

When a wife has that giving attitude toward her husband, that husband is a blessed man!

When a husband has that giving attitude toward his wife, that wife is a blessed woman!

A third thing happens when you base your sex life on godly principles: you have a built-in marriage counselor in God's Word. If you need more information about how to be a good sexual partner to your spouse, go to the Song of Solomon. You'll find all kinds of inspiration and education in that book! If you don't understand all that is written there, get yourself a good commentary on that book. You'll learn some things that your spouse will be glad you learned!

If you need to change some of the bad teaching you've received about sex or replace with truth some of the lies that the devil has told you about sex or your spouse, go to God's Word. Look up some of these words in a concordance and readjust your thinking and your believing when it comes to sex and sexual behavior:

- Adultery
- Fornication
- Fruitfulness
- Affection
- Faithfulness
- Giving and receiving

Study what God's Word has to say about being a giving, affectionate, generous, undemanding, need-meeting person.

If you struggle in talking to your spouse about sexual matters, or if you and your spouse can't find the answers you need in God's Word, go to a godly counselor. You also may find help in a book about sexual ABCs—I recommend that you find a book that has been written by a Christian.

Don't just hope or wish things might change. Get yourselves some help.

Keep Your Sexual Relationship Exciting

Let me share with you several passages from the Song of Solomon that relate to a key principle for preventing conflict in the bedroom. The first passage is this:

> Behold, you are fair, my love! Behold, you are fair! You have dove's eyes behind your veil. Your hair is like a flock of goats, going down from Mount Gilead. Your teeth are like a flock of shorn sheep which have come up from the washing, every one of which bears twins, and none is barren among them. Your lips are like a strand of scarlet, and your mouth is lovely. Your temples behind your veil are like a piece of pomegranate. Your neck is like the tower of David, built for an armory, on which hang a thousand bucklers, all shields of mighty men. Your two breasts are like two fawns, twins of a gazelle, which feed among the lilies. Until the day breaks and the shadows flee away, I will go my way to the mountain of myrrh and to the hill of frankincense. You are all fair, my love, and there is no spot in you.
>
> (Song of Solomon 4:1–7)

Now, you may not understand all the symbolism Solomon was using here, but one thing should come through loud and clear: Solomon was in love with this woman. He thought she was beautiful.

She was a delight to him. She was *"fair"* to his eyes; he liked what he saw.

Make Yourself Attractive

One of the greatest helps to a good sex life is "attractiveness." People don't tend to get married unless they are attracted to each other. You may not see that attractiveness in a person's spouse, but you don't have to see it. It's enough that the two people in the marriage found something attractive in each other.

Don't lose your attractiveness. Work at maintaining it. There's no excuse for becoming a dirty slob. There's no excuse for walking around in a tattered old house robe, slopping around in fuzzy house slippers, with curlers piled up on your head. There's no excuse for wearing a torn old T-shirt, some gym shorts, and smelly tennis shoes, with a toothpick hanging out of your mouth.

Solomon also wrote,

> *How much better than wine is your love, and the scent of your perfumes than all spices! Your lips, O my spouse, drip as the honeycomb; honey and milk are under your tongue; and the fragrance of your garments is like the fragrance of Lebanon.* (Song of Solomon 4:10–11)

There's no excuse for failing to brush your teeth, wash your hair, and take a bath. There's no excuse for having foul breath or body odor. There's no excuse for wearing clothes that smell like the mechanic's shop or the gym.

Choose to look nice and smell nice for your spouse. Get some decent underwear and night wear. Buy yourself some cologne or aftershave. Get yourself some mouthwash. Put some Vaseline or balm on your lips. Give yourself a manicure and pedicure. Keep your hands and feet soft. Shave what needs to be shaved.

Go on a Date

Never stop dating your spouse. Solomon didn't, and he probably had never heard the word *date*. Solomon wrote,

> *Come with me from Lebanon, my spouse, with me from Lebanon. Look from the top of Amana, from the top of*

Senir and Hermon, from the lions' dens, from the mountains of the leopards. (Song of Solomon 4:8)

Occasionally you need to leave the house and go someplace together where the two of you can be alone and be as romantic as you want to be without worrying about the children, the neighbors, or anything else. Take the phone off the hook, or, better yet,

Never stop dating your spouse.

leave the cell phone at home and get away from the house together. Go on a date. Go out together to a romantic restaurant where the lights are low and there are no crying babies demanding to be fed. Go spend a night in a hotel. If you don't have the money to take a trip together, just drive out of town and find a motel in the next county. Do something fun and exciting together.

Spice up your life a bit. Make some new memories.

One time my wife and I went up north, and we had a motel room with a bed that was made like a covered wagon. Pam knows that I love westerns, so she found this motel room that had a big wagon wheel hanging over it. When Pam came out of the bathroom wearing a holster with fake guns and a cowboy hat and very little else, I knew we were going to make some new memories that night!

Flirt with Your Spouse
Solomon wrote,

You have ravished my heart, my sister, my spouse; you have ravished my heart with one look of your eyes, with one link of your necklace. (v. 9)

Notice that Solomon saw this woman first as his sister. He respected her. That's a vitally important concept related to your sexual relationship. You need to see your spouse as God sees your spouse. Husband, you need to see your wife first as your sister in the Lord. Wife, you need to see your husband first as your brother in the Lord. Why? Two reasons. Reason number one is that the Lord loves your spouse with an unconditional love. That's the kind of love you need to have for your spouse; it's the kind of love family members have for one another—parents for children, sisters for brothers, and so forth. Reason number two is that God respects your spouse. God will not violate the free will of your spouse. God doesn't force anybody to do something he or she doesn't want to do. You need to love your spouse in that way.

When you approach your spouse with unconditional love and respect, you can flirt all you want and it won't be vulgar, off-color, or offensive. And believe me, flirtation is what is going on in this passage. With just a look from this woman's eyes and with the way she tilted her head or glanced over her shoulder at him, he was getting a message!

Continue to flirt with your spouse. Continue to wear what he likes to see. Continue to use makeup to enhance your best features. Husband, you do the same. Continue to treat your spouse with romance. Buy those flowers, bring home that red rose, leave that little love note, play that music that she knows as "your song," remember that anniversary. Drop little hints from morning to night that say, "I love you, I want you, I can hardly wait to be with you."

Do you know what your spouse likes to see you wear? If you don't, ask him! Find out your spouse's favorite color, styles, and hem lengths.

Occasionally, it's fun to dress up. My wife and I have Jane and Tarzan outfits. Now, we certainly don't wear those outfits out in public, but we can have fun wearing those outfits in the privacy of our own bedroom!

Set the Stage for Romance

Romance doesn't end when the honeymoon is over. That's the time it should be beginning! Solomon wrote,

> Awake, O north wind, and come, O south! Blow upon my garden, that its spices may flow out. Let my beloved come to his garden and eat its pleasant fruits.
>
> (Song of Solomon 4:16)

Solomon was speaking of the winds of passion. Do whatever it is that sets the stage for your spouse to feel relaxed, beautiful or handsome, and sexy. Light those candles. Turn on that soft music.

Make your spouse feel as if he or she is the luckiest person in the world. Sprinkle some rose petals on the bed. Be creative in planning special moments that honor your spouse and make your spouse feel as if he or she is the luckiest person in the world to be married to you.

Resolving Conflict in the Bedroom

The first thing you need to do when you sense there is a sexual conflict in your marriage is to take an objective look at the problem. We tend to respond emotionally when the issue of sex is raised. Step back and try to be more objective.

If your spouse is bringing up repeatedly the same suggestions or criticisms, or if your spouse is making the same statements about what he or she desires, take note of that. There's a problem! Get to the core of it. Talk to your spouse about the problem. Define the problem as best you can.

Then, take a look at yourself. Don't launch into accusations against your spouse. Don't be critical of your spouse. And, by all means, don't give up on your relationship. This is a problem, and problems have solutions. Needs can be met. Compromises usually can be reached. Decisions can be made. Actions and attitudes can change. Start with yourself in examining what you think and feel and how you are speaking and behaving.

Ask yourself, "Is there something wrong with *my* thinking? Is there something I'm not doing that I should do? Is there something I'm doing that I should stop doing?"

Forgive your spouse if you believe your spouse has offended you. Recognize that, in some cases, your spouse may never have been taught some of the basics of hygiene, romance, or sexual behavior. Some people may have been taught a negative perspective on sex. Some may have had terrible role models when it comes to how men and women treat each other sexually. As you forgive your spouse, forgive those who have taught your spouse incorrectly.

Then, talk over solutions with your spouse. Come to an agreement. Risk being vulnerable in your communication. Bring up the difficult issue.

With your spouse, revisit what God's Word says about a good sexual relationship.

If you have an unsaved spouse, you may have to say to him or her, "I don't believe that is the right thing to do." If your spouse continues to require certain sexual behavior of you that you genuinely believe is contrary to God's Word, then you need to intercede in prayer for your spouse, but you also need to stand firm in your convictions. If he or she doesn't change, if he or she desires to leave the marriage, or if you can't come to some sort of agreement and compromise, then so be it. Never go beyond what you know to be right before God.

Let me be specific here. I once had a woman come to me and say, "My husband is unsaved. He wants to try swapping marriage partners with a particular couple who suggested this to him. He got angry with me for not going along with his idea. Am I supposed to submit to what he wants?" No. What that husband wants is for that wife to commit adultery. There's no provision in God's Word for her to commit adultery and still be in favor with God. Hebrews 13:4 is very clear on this: *"Fornicators and adulterers God will judge."*

On the other hand, if your unsaved spouse tells you that he (or she) would like to have sex four times a week and you as a saved person want to have sex only two times a month, don't blame your lack of sexual desire on God. God's Word has no prescriptions for how many times a month a married couple should have sex. You need to reach a compromise with your spouse.

What about Pornography?

Some people, usually men, like to look at pornography to arouse themselves sexually. Some couples get into watching pornographic films. One couple told me one time, "We were virgins when we got married. We started watching these films to learn what to do. But now we can't seem to stop watching the films."

Let me say four things very briefly about pornography. First, it's ungodly. Much of pornography is related to fornication, adultery, homosexuality, self-gratification, and sadomasochistic behavior (whips, chains, control, inflicting pain). All those behaviors are off-limits according to God's Word!

Pornography is created by ungodly people who regard sex as a means of controlling or manipulating others. God never intended sex to be a means of manipulation or control.

Pornography may be instructive, but it's not instructive about things you should seek to be instructed in! Actually, in most cases, pornography is titillating and not at all instructive. There's a huge difference between something being instructive, which tells "how to"; and titillating, which instills feelings of "got to." Pornography creates in a person a "drive" toward sexual behavior that is *not* what God designed. That's why it's ungodly. You don't need to go to pornographic films or magazines or websites to learn about sex. Enjoy each other. Talk about what you might like to try together. Talk about what turns you on and makes you feel fulfilled sexually. Don't invite outside images into your bedroom.

Second, pornography sets up a false image of comparison. People in magazines and films in all likelihood bear no resemblance whatsoever to your spouse. It is unlikely that they are godly people. They are models and actors. If you start expecting your spouse to "appear" or "perform" in the way these models and actors appear or perform, you are setting yourself up for great disappointment and frustration. You and your spouse have *your* marriage—nobody else's. Keep these outside competitors out of your minds.

Third, pornography is nearly always rooted in selfishness—in a selfish need to have others do your bidding, in a selfish need to have your own needs met regardless of what another person needs, in a selfish need to be in charge all the time. The godly man or woman seeks to be a giver, not a self-centered control freak!

Fourth, pornography is addictive. A little pornography tends to create a desire for more pornography. Don't get started with "soft porn." You'll be opening up yourself and your marriage to all sorts of evil spirits and influences.

Keep pornography out of your home completely. Don't let it in the door. No magazines, no videos, no porn cable stations on your television, no porn websites. Keep yourselves pure.

Have Fun Together

Sex is serious, but you don't always need to be serious in your sexual relationship. Laugh together. Tease. Fantasize together. Play games together.

Don't let your whole life become so serious that you can't have a little fun.

The more you have fun together, the more fun you are going to want to have together!

15

Resolving Conflicts Related to Children

❖❖❖

I will put My trust in Him....Here am I and the children whom God has given Me.
—Hebrews 2:13

The last thing God wants is for our children to dictate what goes on in a household or family. The last thing God wants is for children to drive a wedge between parents or cause one spouse to side with a child against another spouse. The last thing God wants is for children to bring embarrassment or shame to parents.

Time and again, however, I encounter couples whose main area of conflict is a child.

Sometimes the child is rebellious.

Sometimes the problem is that one parent has favored the child over the spouse. Let me be very clear at the outset of this chapter: the bond between spouses is intended to surpass the bond between parent and child. Parents give birth to children, children grow and leave home, and parents remain. A spouse's first loyalty must always be to his or her spouse, not to a child.

> A spouse's first loyalty must always be to his or her spouse, not to a child.

Within that context of united parents, the Bible has very clear teaching about how parents are to teach their children the commands and truths of God, not only by what they say, but also by how they relate to each other.

God's Word says,

> When I was my father's son, tender and the only one in the sight of my mother, he also taught me, and said to me: "Let your heart retain my words; keep my commands, and live."
> (Proverbs 4:3–4)

Any time parents manifest behavior that is contrary to God's words, those parents are teaching their children something contrary to God's commands and are setting an example of sin, which leads to death. The opposite is also true: parents who teach by their example the commands of God are teaching their children concepts that will lead to life.

This is an awesome privilege and responsibility for every parent. If parents display conflict between themselves, they are teaching conflict to their children. If a husband and wife mistreat each other, they are teaching their children that marriage is an environment in which mistreatment is permissible.

The way you treat your spouse is the most potent lesson your child will ever have in how to conduct him- or herself in relationship to other people, including how to relate to his or her own spouse one day. The atmosphere you create in your marriage and in your home will be the atmosphere your children "learn," and it will be the atmosphere they later establish in their own marriages and homes.

The way you treat your spouse is the most potent lesson your child will ever have.

The conflict that a rebellious, sinful child creates in a family comes from *somewhere*. The first place to look is the environment you created for that child early in his or her life. Now, that truth isn't shared with you to bring condemnation to you, but rather to reinforce how important it is that parents take full responsibility for creating the environment in the home.

Resolving Conflicts Related to Children

Establishing a Godly Environment

According to God's Word, the father takes the responsibility for guiding and directing his children. Too many couples leave the "child rearing" to the mother. It is a father's role to establish an environment of respect, consideration, and love in the home. He does this by treating the child's mother with respect, consideration, and love. He does this by speaking to his wife in a tone that is kind, protective, and affectionate. If the husband does not manifest respect for his spouse, he cannot expect respect from his child for either the mother or himself! A father is teaching his children not only how to respect and love their mother, but also how to respect and love him as their father.

If your child hears you apologize to each other, your child is going to learn that it's entirely acceptable to say, "I'm sorry; please forgive me."

If your child sees you crying or showing tender emotion in the presence of your spouse, your child is going to learn that it's a good thing to be vulnerable to a spouse and that there's nothing wrong with showing tender feelings or sorrow.

If your child sees you trusting your spouse and speaking well of your spouse's accomplishments and behavior, your child is going to learn that people can be trusted and that a spouse should be built up and acknowledged.

When a child sees his or her parents relating to each other in kindness and affection, that child has a sense of security. Nothing gives a child greater security than the knowledge that his or her parents love each other.

The opposite is also true. If your child sees you arguing and fighting all the time, a child develops a sense of insecurity. And he or she will act out that insecurity in negative ways—from tantrums to withdrawal to outright rebellion.

The father who demeans a child's mother or abuses a child's mother causes that child to demean and abuse his or her mother, as well as to demean and abuse the father.

A mother's role is to complete the father's guidance by giving specific instructions and directions that are built on the foundation established by the father. She adds the practical how-tos and the procedures that need to be followed in order to implement the father's plans regarding how the family is going to function.

In summary, a father sets the principles. The mother sets the procedures that put the principles into action.

A great deal of conflict will arise in children if this pattern is not followed, and that conflict will come flying squarely back into the

A father sets the principles. A mother sets the procedures.

faces of the father and mother. "That's your son." "No, that's *your* son." "Well, if you were the type of father that child needs...." "What do you mean? You're the mother. You're the one who's there in the home most of the time." You've heard all the arguments. As a pastor, I'm standing there saying, "This is the son of both of you, and you have a mutual responsibility for creating the right environment for your child! Get your parental roles in line with God's Word, and a great deal of this conflict is going to disappear."

Structuring Your Child's Peer Relationships

Your child's friends are *your* responsibility. You and your spouse need to come to agreement about who will be the friends of your children. It's not your child's responsibility to choose his or her friends. It's your responsibility as the parents.

A great deal of conflict in families could be prevented if parents would take a more active role in choosing friends for their

Your child's friends are *your* responsibility.

children. Proverbs 13:20 says, *"He who walks with wise men will be wise, but the companion of fools will be destroyed."* Don't let your children run the streets. Know where your children are, who they are with, and what they are doing.

Get to know your child's acquaintances at school, on the playground, in the sports teams and social clubs, and at the church. The more you get to know the peers of your child, the better you will be able to guide your child toward those friendships that are nurturing and positive and away from those that have strong potential for bringing destruction. Tell your children why you think some friendships would be good for them to cultivate. Tell them why you are forbidding them to associate with some people.

Now, I'm not at all advocating that you criticize your child's friends all the time. No, sometimes it's enough to say, "I'm not in favor of your spending time at that child's house. I don't know their parents well enough. I have some concerns about what goes on in their family." If you have established the right home atmosphere for your child, your child knows there's something not quite right about another child's home life or his or her attitude. Your child doesn't need a detailed psychological profile of all that is wrong with that friend.

At other times, it's better to ask your child, "Why do you like that person as your friend?" Ask questions about the behavioral manifestations that are of concern to you. "Does it bother you that your friend...?" "Are you concerned that your friend...?" "What do you think you might be able to do to help your friend...?"

If your child walks with wise individuals, your child will be wise. If your child walks with foolish individuals, he or she will be destroyed.

Issues You Need to Discuss

There are several issues that you need to discuss before marriage with the person you are intending to marry. If you didn't discuss these issues before you got married, you certainly need to discuss them now!

The Decision to Bear Children

Do you intend to have children together? How many children should you have? These are issues you should discuss before you get married.

Don't go into a marriage with a person who doesn't want to have children if you desire to have five children. Don't marry somebody who can't produce children if you have had a lifelong desire to have children of your own. Discuss the issue of adoption and foster parenting with your spouse. If you have a desire to have children but you can't conceive a child of your own, are you willing to explore these other options?

Also discuss the issue of abortion. Does your spouse think that it's right to abort a child that you conceive together? If so, there are some serious issues you need to face. Find out why your spouse holds that opinion. If your spouse believes it's right to kill your offspring, you are going to find that your spouse is also likely to be angry at *you* any time child rearing becomes a challenge or you go through a rough time with a child.

The number of children you have is also something you should continue to discuss until your childbearing days are over. Some people go into marriage wanting several children, but after the birth of one or two children, they know they have completed their family. Some women are not able to bear more than one child. Some people develop medical problems that make conception very difficult or impossible.

Keep in mind that the issue of childbearing is not part of the marriage vow. Never say in anger or disgust to your spouse, "You promised to have three children, and now you want to stop after having only two." If your spouse says something like that to you, don't get angry. Get a third person involved—perhaps a medical doctor or a pastoral counselor—to help you work through the issue.

Also face the issue that God determines the sex of your child. Don't say to your spouse, "I want to keep having babies until we have a baby of the gender I want." That's pure selfishness.

Never blame your spouse for having a boy or a girl, as if your spouse could determine that in advance! For centuries, men have blamed women for a failure to "give them a son." Husband, it's your sperm that determines the sex of a child! If you are going to make one person responsible for determining the sex of your baby, it has to be the man!

Birth Control

Decide prior to your marriage what kind of birth control you are going to use. Continue to discuss that issue all through your childbearing years. You may start out using birth control and then decide not to use any birth control devices. Or you may start out with no birth control and decide to use birth control devices later in your marriage. Talk it over.

If you choose to use birth control, make sure that you both are committed to the method you use. Husband, don't hide your wife's birth control pills in hopes that you can get your wife pregnant. Don't fail to use a condom if that's the method of birth control you have chosen as a couple to use. Wife, don't forget to take your birth control pills. Don't forget to use a device that the two of you have agreed to use. This is a matter of being trustworthy to your spouse.

The Discipline of Children

One area of conflict in marriage related to children involves the discipline of the children. Before having children, talk about how you are going to raise your children. Ask the Holy Spirit to reveal to you the most effective form of discipline for each child you have. Some children need a strong hand; other children are so sensitive that a serious, firm word to them will turn them from their error to the way they should go.

God's Word says,

> Do not withhold correction from a child, for if you beat him with a rod, he will not die. You shall beat him with a rod, and deliver his soul from hell.   (Proverbs 23:13–14)

Notice the first part of that passage: *"Do not withhold correction from a child."* You need to tell your children when they are doing something that is wrong before God, wrong in your eyes as parents, and wrong in the eyes of the society in which we live. Any time your child does something that will bring harm to him- or herself, harm to another person, or harm to another person's property, that child needs to be corrected.

Correct your child in terms your child understands and to which your child responds.

No child ever died from a spanking that was administered in the right way—with the hand of the parent on the buttocks of the child. What does the Bible mean by a *"rod"* here? That's a reference to the "rod of correction." It's actually a reference to speaking the Word of God to your child.

We all know the phrase that you sometimes have to "beat the truth into a child." Well, that's a very old understanding. A strong verbal administration of the truth is sometimes required. It is not that you are nagging or preaching at your child all the time from the Bible; but rather, when your child makes an error and you punish that child, let that child know exactly what he or she did that was wrong in God's eyes and therefore in your eyes.

Spanking a child doesn't keep a child from going to hell. But punishing a child and simultaneously reinforcing the concepts of right behavior that are in God's Word *will* keep a child from sin.

Discuss this with your spouse. Come to some agreement about who will punish the children and how and when and for what offenses. Set some consequences for the behavior of your children.

Why is this so important?

A home that is ruled by unruly children is a home that is a battleground. If your child's will is the governing force in your home, you as parents will be extremely frustrated, and in your frustration, you will experience conflict with each other.

The Training of Your Children

Training a child means far more than disciplining or punishing a child. It means finding out what your child can do and helping your child succeed in his or her natural talents. Discover all the capabilities and positive traits that God built into your child. Help your child strengthen those traits and develop those abilities into skills. Set your child up for practical success in life.

Training means setting restrictions and boundaries. Training means teaching your child God's commandments and insisting that he or she abide by them. Make the rules of your home very clear: no cheating, no stealing, no staying home from church, no lying, no skipping school. Establish consequences for a failure to keep the rules you establish as parents.

In doing this, you are teaching your children to respect authority—not only your authority as parents, but also the authority they will face as they enter the workplace and the culture at large.

Training means teaching your child to take responsibility for his or her own actions. It means teaching your child the value of work, the best way to manage money, and the basic rules of hygiene and grooming. When one of our sons was young, he decided that he no longer needed to wear clean clothes, bathe, or comb his hair and brush his teeth. One day I took him to the dictionary, opened it to the word *bum,* and made him read the definition aloud to me. I announced to his mother and brother, "We have a bum in our house. Bums don't have television, they don't have warm beds, they don't have nice clothes or toys. They tend to live under bridges and sleep on park benches. They don't associate much with other people because bums smell bad. They certainly don't eat at dining tables with people who are clean and well groomed. I think the time has come for the bum in our house to live in the basement to see what his future as a bum is going to be like."

Now, we had a fully finished basement that had a bed in it, so there was no harsh abuse involved in what we were teaching our son. We sent our "bum" to sleep in the basement, and we took him a small tray of dinner. We insisted that he wear the same clothes day and night. We took away his comb and toothbrush.

It only took a couple of days before our "bum" decided that he didn't want to be a bum. He learned a valuable lesson in less than seventy-two hours—and it's a lesson that has stuck with him to this day.

Find creative ways to get your children not only to understand the rules you set for them, but also to appreciate the reasoning behind those rules and the benefits for keeping the rules, as well as the consequences for breaking them. Point out to them examples of what happens to people who keep God's commandments and examples of the consequences experienced by those who don't keep them.

The Role of the Grandparents

It's up to you and your spouse to determine the role that each of your parents will have in your children's lives. Grandparents can be your greatest allies, or they can be your greatest enemies in the raising of your children. If your parents are speaking against your spouse to your children, they are going to be a voice for disrespect and conflict in your home. If your parents go against the rules that you and your spouse have established for your children, they are going to be a voice for rebellion and conflict.

Have an understanding between yourselves about how you intend to relate to both sets of grandparents, as well as the degree to which you want both sets of grandparents to be involved in your family and in the lives of your children.

Then, out of that understanding, go to each set of grandparents and let them know the ground rules that you have established for your home and for the raising of your children. If they agree to cooperate with your agenda and follow through and support what you are attempting to do for your children, great! If they fail to go along with your agenda or they contradict what you are attempting to teach your children, then keep your children away from those grandparents or monitor closely the time spent with them.

A Word about Stepparents

If you are a single parent and you are thinking about marrying, talk to your children about your intentions. Don't just assume they will fall in line with what you want. They have their own feelings of rejection, bitterness, and anger to deal with over the absence of a father or mother in their lives, and they will have their own response to the introduction of a stepparent. Explain, discuss, and share what you are deciding and planning. Get their response. Talk about ways you hope your family can function in a positive, godly way.

If you are anticipating bringing a spouse into a family that you have already created as a single or divorced parent, you need to have some serious conversations with that future stepparent about your children, about the way they have been raised thus far, and about the way you hope they will be raised in the future. If you don't have agreement on the way you are going to raise the children you already have in your life, don't marry that person. Don't be so eager to get a person into your family that you ignore, overlook, or shortchange the people who are already in your family!

It's wrong for you to bring a person into your child's life and make your child feel as if he or she has to compete for your love and attention. Put yourself into your child's shoes. How would you feel if someone suddenly was brought into your home and you were told that this virtual stranger had authority over you, even though he or she had never taken any responsibility for you prior to that day? How would you feel if you suddenly were asked to obey a person and you had no idea what rules he or she expected you to obey? How would you feel if suddenly you were subjected to discipline from a person you hardly knew?

Don't push your child into a relationship your child may not want to have. Don't ask your child to call a stepparent "Mama" or "Daddy."

Long before you think about getting married and introducing a stepparent into your child's world, spend time with that potential future stepparent and your child *together*. See how everybody relates to one another. Build a relationship. If a relationship doesn't take root, don't get married. If your child doesn't bond with the person you want to have as his or her stepparent, you are inviting big-time conflict into your life. The conflict will flow in all directions, including conflict between you and your spouse.

If the man or woman you are dating doesn't want to spend time with your children, consider that a huge red flag. Find someone to date who does want to be around your children.

Children Are a Blessing

The Bible calls children a blessing. They will be a blessing to you if you choose to bless them by being godly spouses to each other and by being godly parents to them.

One of the greatest ways you can bless your child is to praise your child often and genuinely. Compliment your child. Acknowledge your child's successes. Reward his or her hard effort. Praise your child's character in the presence of others.

There's no greater reward on this earth than to have children who love God and love you. Bless your child's individuality. Don't stifle his or her creativity; rather, find a way to channel it into positive activities and expressions. Don't compare your child to his or her siblings. Be openly appreciative of the unique qualities that make your child special.

The more you bless your child in these ways, the more your child will be a blessing. There's no greater reward on this earth than to have children who love God and love you.

16

Resolving Conflicts Related to Money

The Lord is my shepherd; I shall not want.
—Psalm 23:1

A man I knew a number of years ago used to say with great dramatic flair, "Rooooomance…without fiiiiinance…is a nuuuuuuisance."

He was right.

The number-one cause of marital conflict is finances—not sex, not children, but money.

God certainly knew this. Money is where the rubber hits the road. It's the most practical part of marriage. And more verses in the Bible deal with the handling of money than just about any other practical subject. Dozens of passages deal with God's ideals regarding money. God wants us to prosper, He wants us to be good stewards of what He entrusts to us, He wants us to deal with finances honestly, and He wants us to live free of debt and free of greed. When we fail to follow God's principles, we always struggle and suffer.

> **Money is the most practical part of marriage.**

Money is at the very heart of many divorces and serious marital conflicts. It's been that way for thousands of years.

191

If I ask a group why Samson lost his strength, most people say, "Because Delilah cut his hair." But if I ask them, "What was Delilah's motivation for cutting Samson's hair?" they have no answer. The answer is *money.* The Bible says that the lords of the Philistines came to Delilah and said, *"Entice him, and find out where his great strength lies, and by what means we may over-power him, that we may bind him to afflict him; and every one of us will give you eleven hundred pieces of silver"* (Judges 16:5).

Don't lose your financial strength; don't fall prey to the devil's lies to conduct your finances in any way other than God's way.

Take Control of Your Finances

We need money to meet our needs. The Bible says, *"Money answers everything"* (Ecclesiastes 10:19). Money buys all we need from the material world. We *need* to have sufficient income to pay our bills.

Ask your spouse, "What do you think about money? What are we working for? What are we going to do with the money that comes into our hands?"

Answer these basic questions, and set your priorities as a couple. Determine how you will use money to improve the quality of your life together.

Whose Money Is It?

In this day and age, with so many husbands and wives work-ing, the prevailing attitude seems to be that the husband's money is his money and the wife's money is her money. I do not believe that's scriptural. The Bible says that when you are married, you are one flesh. "One flesh" is not only a term related to sexual union; it's also a term that means *together* the two of you are one physical entity in society. You are one family. You are one budget and one source of spending. You are one household. You share a corner of the material world with a mutuality of interest, concern, and care.

Discuss this with your spouse. Ask yourself, "What are we going to do with *our* money?" Reach an understanding about your shared financial goals, principles, and limits on spending.

Help each other to be disciplined in this area of your life.

There was a time early in our marriage when Pamela and I were on welfare. I had been struck by lightning and was seriously injured and unable to work. We needed the temporary financial assistance that was available to us in the form of welfare.

We knew that in living on a welfare check, there were certain things that we could not purchase. So we didn't purchase them! We didn't dwell on all the things we couldn't purchase. We focused on the things we could buy.

We had to discipline ourselves. We got used to living on generic foods and using generic products. Back in those days, generic brands tended to be black ink on white paper: Tea. Soda. Tissue. Crackers. Salt. You could have taught a child to read and spell just by opening our cupboards. We came to an understanding, however, that we could not afford anything other than generic foods, so we did not tempt ourselves by shopping in stores where we couldn't afford to buy anything. We didn't go the mall and just roam around looking at stuff. We didn't drive through neighborhoods where we couldn't afford to live. When you continually surround yourselves with the images of things that you can't afford, you become jealous and discontent.

When you face your limits and choose to live within your limits, you generally can find a way to meet your basic needs and even save something within those limits. You can find a way to be creative with your cooking, with your spending, with your decorating, and with your clothing.

As long as I had control of our family checkbook, we were broke. One day God said to me, "Let Pam keep the checkbook. Let her keep track of the family finances."

What happened when I obeyed what God told me to do in this area of our marriage? We started prospering! We started having money in the bank. We had a checkbook that was balanced.

I gained understanding that I didn't need to control our family's finances. I came to understand that my wife is a better money manager than I am—I have a tendency to give away or spend every penny that comes our way. Pam has a tendency to be generous and still invest and save some of what comes our way.

I also came to understand that there were some things in our marriage that I didn't have to do just because other men in my family and in my culture did them. I could do what God told me to do. And I discovered that when I chose to do what God told me to do, my life improved. So did our marriage.

Analyze Your Assets and Liabilities

"I don't have any assets." I've had countless people feed me that line. The truth of God is that you do have assets. Everybody has personal assets—your clothing, your jewelry, your other personal "stuff." Your house and your car are assets. Your goal in financial management should be to build up your assets and reduce your liabilities, which are your debts, so that you increase your "net worth." The math is very simple. Add up the value of all you have. Subtract all you owe. The resulting answer is your net worth.

"Well, we can't count on being alive tomorrow. Who knows? We might die tonight. I don't care about having any savings or a 'net worth' for the future." Let me respond this way: You may die tonight. But you also may live another fifty years. If you live another fifty years, who's going to take care of you? Who is going to run your life? Who is going to determine where you go and how much you can spend? If you don't plan in a way that will allow you to take care of yourselves in the future, you'll lose your personal freedom, and your quality of life will greatly decrease.

Face Your Indebtedness

Discuss issues of money, debt, and credit before you get married. Are you about to marry someone with a pile of debt who is anticipating that he or she will pay that debt using your money and your good credit rating? Know that before you get that joint checking account!

Make a Budget Together

From the very outset of your marriage, you need to have a budget to which you both agree. Then you need to spend within that budget. If you will do that one thing—live according to a budget—you'll prevent 90 percent of the financial conflict that most people experience in their marriages.

Take a look at your income. Then take a look at your expenses—all of them. Start with the basics. As far as I'm concerned, the first portion of your income that should be set aside as a basic expense is your tithe to the church. Get God's blessings on the other part of your money by putting God first. If you

> You can prevent 90 percent of the conflict most people experience in marriage.

need to know more about this, go to Malachi 3:8–11. Read every word of that passage until you get the concept deep in your spirit. God honors what is given to Him. He pours out a blessing on your life and rebukes evil from your life.

In times past, a man didn't ask for a woman's hand in marriage until he could provide for her totally on the basis of his own income. In some cultures, a man not only had to have a steady job, but he also had to have a house. He had to show his future wife's parents that he could support her and any children who might be born to the marriage.

In today's world, with so many women working, there's less emphasis on a husband being able to provide for his wife. But let me tell you this—according to God's Word, the provision and protection of a wife is a husband's responsibility. The wife may want to work, she may have a good job, the two may agree that they both will work and earn and spend the family money, or the husband

> The husband has the responsibility for provision and protection of his wife and children.

and wife may want to be in business or in ministry together, but the bottom line is that the husband has the responsibility for provision and protection of his wife and children.

Certainly there may be exceptions to that—for example, cases where the husband becomes sick or disabled or in cases where a husband is laid off and has difficulty finding employment. But there's no justification based on God's Word for a lazy man to be supported by a working wife.

The Bible says,

> *If anyone will not work, neither shall he eat. For we hear that there are some who walk among you in a disorderly manner, not working at all, but are busybodies. Now those who are such we command and exhort through our Lord Jesus Christ that they work in quietness and eat their own bread.* (2 Thessalonians 3:10–12)

Paul said about his time spent among the Thessalonians,

> *We were not disorderly among you; nor did we eat anyone's bread free of charge, but worked with labor and toil night and day, that we might not be a burden to any of you, not because we do not have authority, but to make ourselves an example of how you should follow us.* (vv. 7–9)

Set Goals for Yourselves

Set some goals for yourselves regarding what you will earn and spend.

Earning Goals

If you aren't making the kind of money you want to make, do something about it. Go back to school or to a training program to get yourself some skills so you can move into a better job. Ask God to open up a new opportunity for you; ask Him to lead you to a better position or a new employer. At your job, do your best. Give 100 percent of your effort and ability. Put yourself into a position to get a raise or a promotion. Stick with that good job—don't slack off. Get some seniority in the company.

Giving Goals

One of the major decisions you and your spouse need to make is how you will *give.* As a Christian, you are commanded to give the tithe and offerings to God's storehouse. As a Christian, you should also have a desire to give. Your motivation for giving may lie in obedience, thanksgiving for all God has given you, the promise of God's reward, or all three! (See Luke 6:38.) Whatever your motivation, give!

Giving brings a blessing to your life; and when you have a life that is blessed materially, you remove a good many obstacles and conflicts.

Make a decision about how you will give, how much you will give, and where you will give. Determine how you will give your money, as well as donate your time, talents, and skills to various fund-raising causes associated with God's work. I recently heard about a man who donates four "concerts" a year to his church. He is a professional pianist, and his church "uses" his talents for a major fund-raising dinner each fall, a ladies' fund-raising tea each spring, and patriotic and Christmas concerts for which tickets are sold in July and December. He is part of the fund-raising fabric of that church. And he tithes on top of that!

Savings and Investing Goals

"A good man leaves an inheritance to his children's children" (Proverbs 13:22). There's only one way to leave an inheritance to your children and grandchildren, and that is to save and invest some of what you earn!

Cars get old, clothes get old, and styles change—but money in the bank does not get old. Every investment may not be a great one, but it's better to invest money than to squander money.

The Bible says, *"Wisdom is a defense as money is a defense"* (Ecclesiastes 7:12). Money gives you a feeling of security; it builds a wall of defense against you and the bill collectors.

The Hebrew word for defense has also been translated as "shade." Money provides a "shade" for your family. It keeps you from the heat of the pressure associated with debt. It keeps you from the heated words of bill collectors. It keeps you from the angry words in your marriage when the money is tight or mis-spent. When money is insufficient in a marriage and the bills are piled up, it's easy for a spouse to become angry. He or she may feel betrayed by the spending behavior or lack of work on the part of the spouse, or a spouse may become frustrated and angry at his or her own lack of discipline and ability when it comes to earning and spending. Too much heat, and your marriage can suffer from heat stroke!

When there's too much heat, a mirage can develop. People start seeing things that aren't real. They become suspicious. They misinterpret behavior. They question every action.

Remove some of the heat. Get yourself a savings and investment plan.

Develop a Spending Plan

A sound approach to your spending can be summed up in **Give some to God, save some, and spend some.** this simple statement: give some to God, save some, and spend some. Our problem is that too many of us are giving nothing to God, saving nothing, and spending a lot. In many cases, we are spending more than we have.

One of the main challenges you will face regarding your spending of money is this: differentiating between needs and wants. Discuss with your spouse those things that you consider to be needs. Differentiate them from your wants. Make sure you are paying for the practical and financial needs of your family before you get into the area of wants.

Pay Your Debts

Ask God to reveal to you a plan for getting your bills paid and for getting out of debt. Take a look at what you have around you. What do you own and perhaps need to sell? What talents and skills do you have that you need to start using? What work can you do and do you need to start doing? Trust God to reveal to you all that you can do to get free of the debt that pulls you down, holds you back, and wears you out in your spirit. (Read the story in 2 Kings 4:1–7; God gave a miracle plan to a woman so she could pay her debts and keep her sons out of bondage. What God did in the past, He does today!)

Debt is an oppressor. It pulls you down in your spirit. God's Word says, *"The rich rules over the poor, and the borrower is servant to the lender"* (Proverbs 22:7). Debt puts you into slavery. It binds your spirit even as it limits your freedom to go and do and purchase what you desire.

The Bible says, *"Owe no one anything except to love one another"* (Romans 13:8).

Recognize that the way out of just about any financial problem you face is the behavior opposite to what got you into the problem.

For example, if overspending your budget is the way you got into a financial crisis, then underspending your budget is the way out of it. Spend *less* than what you think you need to spend and use what's left to pay against the principal on your credit cards, loans, or overdue bills.

If neglecting to pay bills on time has created a financial problem for you, then start paying your bills early. There was a time early in our marriage when Pamela and I had a large amount of debt. We would have liked to have put those bills in a drawer and opened the drawer two weeks later to see those bills gone. That never happened. We had to face up to the fact that bills need to be paid.

We sat down and made a detailed plan about how we were going to get out of debt. Then we called every creditor we had and told them what we could do every month. We sent every creditor *something* every month. We started making extra payments on the bill that was the biggest. When we got that bill paid off, it was a great feeling! We used what we had been paying on that bill every month to pay extra on the next-largest bill. It got paid off even quicker. We felt like we were on a roll. The more bills we paid off, the more we added that amount every month to another bill. Within three years, we were debt-free.

> The way out of financial problems is the behavior opposite to what got you there.

Two things happened along the way. One, we found ourselves motivated to stay out of debt once we got out of debt. Some folks pay off a bill and then say to themselves, "Well, I have a little extra money now. I think I'll spend it on something I want." That's a dangerous pattern. Use that amount you were paying on a bill to increase what you can pay against another bill. And once you get out of debt, do your best to stay out of debt. Debt is a bondage.

The second thing that happened was that we found ourselves sleeping better at night once we got out of debt. There's a peace of mind and a feeling of freedom and security that come with knowing you have a little money in the bank rather than a stack of bills you can't pay.

Show me a husband and wife who have their bills paid and a little money saved, and I'll show you a couple who have very few conflicts regarding finances in their marriage. And in most cases, that couple also will have fewer conflicts in other areas of their lives together. Conflicts about money create an anxiety and a lack of security that spill over into other areas of the marriage. There's more anxiety and less security about a spouse's faithfulness and the degree to which a spouse can be trusted; there's more anxiety and less security regarding your children and what you can provide for them now and in the future; there's more anxiety and less security regarding your health (especially if there's no money to pay for doctor bills, medicines, or health insurance). Deal with the money issue, and you probably will have dealt with other issues before they could become issues!

Learn How to Manage Money

People aren't born knowing how to manage money wisely. They have to learn to manage money.

If you have never learned how to manage money, work with somebody who can teach you how to manage your finances. If you don't know how to invest money wisely, talk to somebody who has invested money wisely. Don't be too proud to learn. Humble yourself and ask questions.

Are you aware that the average millionaire goes broke or bankrupt three times before he makes his fortune? Millionaires are people who are willing to take a risk to try to get ahead, and when they make mistakes and fail, they pick themselves up and try again.

Part of learning how to manage money is learning how to keep financial records. Keep your finances organized. Keep track of what you earn and spend.

Organization starts with a budget, but it doesn't end there. Too many people have said, "What I don't know won't hurt me." The fact is, if you don't know where your money is going, you are probably going to get hurt! Keep financial records. Know where your money is going.

Record keeping is a part of accountability. It's part of building trust in a relationship.

Guard Your Use of Credit Cards

Another problem that we have in today's marriages is the use of credit cards. It's easy to buy something "on loan" when you don't really have the money in your hand. Are you aware that when you use a credit card, you are taking out a loan to make a purchase? You will have to pay back that loan usually within thirty days to avoid paying interest on it. And if you're late making that loan payment to the credit card company, you'll find yourself paying late fees on top of the interest! That's crazy! Before long, you're in debt and in conflict.

Get free of those credit cards. Lay aside your credit cards for emergencies, not for every trip to town or to the mall. Pay cash. What you save in interest and late fees is money you can put into a savings account or into investments. The money you save will **Get free of those credit cards.** grow, and before long you'll have a little financial security to replace your financial worry.

Don't put more on your credit card than you can afford to pay off in a month or two. You'll end up with high interest charges, and, in the end, if you make only a "minimum payment," you may find you are paying two and three times as much for an item by the time you add up all the interest.

Confront Your Attitude about Money

If you have nothing left over after giving your tithe, paying your taxes, setting aside something for savings, and paying your basic bills for food, shelter, transportation, clothing, and other necessities, well, so be it. You will just eat, sleep, and live! That's all that

99.99 percent of the world does! Don't feel deprived. Feel blessed that God is providing for your needs.

Confront Selfishness

One of the greatest sources of financial conflict is rooted in selfishness. One or both people in the marriage think in terms of what *I* want to spend rather than what *we* want to spend. Without any advance discussion or planning, the selfish person goes to the store and buys what he or she wants to buy without any consideration of the spouse, the family budget, or the agreement that has been made regarding how the family money is going to be spent.

A person who does this is not only selfish, but also untrustworthy. If you tell your spouse that you are going to live within the budget you have mutually established, and then you don't live within it, you are living a lie. How can your spouse trust you with his or her secrets, dreams, and goals if he or she can't trust you with the checkbook? How can your spouse count on you to be there in good times and bad if he or she can't count on you to go to the store and not come home with stuff you haven't mutually agreed to buy?

Selfishness always breeds distrust. Distrust, in turn, can lead to anger, frustration, and severe conflict.

Why Do You Feel Deprived?

Ask yourself why you feel deprived when you can't buy everything you want to buy. What has happened to your self-esteem? Why is your self-worth tied up with what you own or how you dress or the kind of watch you have on your wrist?

Most of us aren't deprived of the things we need. Rather, we feel deprived if we don't get the things we want.

Some people feel deprived because they don't get what they want in the very instant they want it. They are impatient.

We live in a world that's geared toward instant gratification. We get upset if our fast-food order isn't ready in sixty seconds. We want to double the money we put into the stock market in a year. We want the latest, newest, and best, and we want it *right now.*

Life doesn't work that way. We grow into prosperity. There may be a season of "waiting" for the harvest. That doesn't mean the harvest isn't going to come. It also doesn't mean that we should be sitting on the edge of our chairs just waiting for the day the harvest comes in. We need to live our lives in contentment and diligent, persistent, hard work, with anticipation of better days ahead.

Confront Your Work Habits

I saw a television spot recently in which a woman was talking about having financial independence, coming into her own financially, developing job-related work skills, and being a working mother. She had her arms spread apart as if she were free and about ready to fly. But then she said something to the effect, "But until I get there, I'm going to use the food stamps provided by the government."

Now, there may be times when you need assistance from someone. I've been in that position. But let me tell you two things plainly. First, you need to see any financial assistance that you receive as *temporary.* That goes for help from Mom and Dad, loans that help you get through school, and any other forms of assistance you receive. God doesn't want you living off food stamps for the rest of your life.

Second, hold on to your dreams about a better life. Don't get discouraged. Keep moving toward those dreams that God places in your heart. Recognize, however, that *work* is the way to get to those dreams. Wishing and hoping won't get you the reality you desire.

Count on plenty of old-fashioned hard work to turn a dream into a reality. There's no prosperity for those who sit down and expect life to hand them a paycheck.

Dealing with Jealousy and Covetousness

Marital conflicts about money are often rooted in jealousy. One or both spouses look at what their neighbors, friends, or other family members own—what they drive, what kind of house they live in, what they wear, what kind of jewelry they are showing off—and they say, "I want that." If you want it, if you can afford it, and if you believe it is part of God's will for you to have it, fine. The conflict comes when you can't afford it. Then the accusations start: "You don't make enough to buy this for me," or "You don't manage the money well enough to save for this," or "You don't spend the money wisely, so we never have enough for this."

Jealousy doesn't kick in on the basics. Very few people are jealous that somebody else has steak instead of hamburger for dinner, that somebody has a nice pair of mittens when there's snow on the ground, or that the electric bill is paid. Jealousy is usually related to "luxury" items—items that are rooted in our wants rather than our needs. Face up to your jealousy.

Choose Contentment

Paul wrote to Timothy,

> Godliness with contentment is great gain. For we brought nothing into this world, and it is certain we can carry nothing out. And having food and clothing, with these we shall be content. But those who desire to be rich fall into temptation and a snare, and into many foolish and harmful lusts which drown men in destruction and perdition. For the love of money is a root of all kinds of evil, for which some have strayed from the faith in their greediness, and pierced themselves through with many sorrows.   (1 Timothy 6:6–10)

Find a level of contentment with what you have. If you pursue money in order to elevate your status and power over other people—in other words, so you might rule over them or impress them—or if you pursue money to try to give yourself feelings of self-esteem or self-worth, or if you pursue money because that is the source of your security and trust—in other words, you trust money more than you trust God—you are in error. The pursuit of money for these reasons can cause a person to fall into all kinds of *"foolish and harmful lusts."*

Find a level of contentment with what you have.

Greed is a form of lust. It's an insatiable desire for more, more, more. A lust for money and more possessions is at the root of all thievery, all financial manipulation, false accounting, and financial cheating. It's at the root of many lies, most frauds, and most deceitful transactions.

Which of You Is the Better Manager?

Early in my marriage, I thought I could handle everything in our relationship related to finances. I thought, *I can earn it, I can spend it, I can account it, I can manage it.* I was wrong.

I learned that my wife, Pamela, is far more disciplined in managing our money, keeping track of it, and investing it. I turned over the financial management of our household to her, and the first of every month, she gives me my "allowance" for the month. That's the money I can spend on things I want to buy.

I admit to you that I have a weakness for shoes. I like to look good when I preach and when I'm not preaching. I especially like good-looking shoes. If it were up to me, I'd probably spend every extra dime I have on shoes. But where would that get me five or ten years from now? I'd have a closet full of shoes—even though I can't wear but one pair at a time. Furthermore, shoe leather wears out. Shoes don't last until retirement. Shoes go out of style. Shoes aren't something you can call "net worth" when you go to the bank in search of a loan for a major investment. I have had to learn to say "no" to my desire for shoes.

I still like shoes. I still buy shoes. But I am increasingly more disciplined in my purchase of shoes. I don't need shoes to make me happy or to give me self-esteem. One of the ways I discipline myself is to stay out of shoe stores! I don't go to the mall on a Monday night just to wander around and tempt myself with shoes.

The Bible says,

> *Honor the LORD with your possessions, and with the first-fruits of all your increase; so your barns will be filled with plenty, and your vats will overflow with new wine.*

> (Proverbs 3:9–10)

The writer of Proverbs was dealing with an agricultural society. The principles are for all of us, however. When we honor the Lord with our possessions and our tithes and offerings, God gives us *increase*. We experience a fullness to our lives, an overflow of blessings, an abundance.

Let me assure you of this: the marriage that gets into overflow and abundance is a marriage that has far fewer conflicts related to money!

17

If We Fail to Resolve Conflict...

✦✦✦

See, I have set before you today life and good, death and evil, in
that I command you today to love the LORD your God, to walk
in His ways, and to keep His commandments...that you may live
and multiply; and the LORD your God will bless you in the land
which you go to possess.
— Deuteronomy 30:15–16

U nresolved conflict always results in the death of something.
If you have unresolved conflict between two nations, you
are going to end up in a bloody war.

By death, I'm not referring to the death of a spouse or to
murder, although in some cases conflict in a marriage has escalated to that point.

I'm talking about the death of respect...

The death of communication...

The death of affection...

The death of family prosperity...

The death of love...

The death of the marriage.

I'm also talking about the death that conflict can create inside
a person:

The death of hope...

The death of self-worth...

The death of faith that God can heal a relationship...

The death of joy...

The death of motivation—including motivation to work on the marriage.

Furthermore, the bigger the conflict, the more difficult it will be for you to bring yourselves to the point of seeking resolution. The bigger the conflict, the harder it will be for you to forgive each other and move on. The bigger the conflict, the more easily trust is destroyed. When trust is destroyed, a house divides.

Unresolved conflict always results in the death of something.

Biblical Grounds for Divorce

Deuteronomy 24 gives the guideline for scriptural divorce in Old Testament times:

> *When a man takes a wife and marries her, and it happens that she finds no favor in his eyes because he has found some uncleanness in her, and he writes her a certificate of divorce, puts it in her hand, and sends her out of his house, when she has departed from his house, and goes and becomes another man's wife, if the latter husband detests her and writes her a certificate of divorce, puts it in her hand, and sends her out of his house, or if the latter husband dies who took her as his wife, then her former husband who divorced her must not take her back to be his wife after she has been defiled; for that is an abomination before the LORD, and you shall not bring sin on the land which the LORD your God is giving you as an inheritance.*
>
> (Deuteronomy 24:1–4)

Many people think the Bible has a great deal to say about divorce. It doesn't. These four verses provided above are the bulk of what the Law of Moses says about divorce. We can determine from these verses that, in Old Testament times:

• Divorce was the prerogative of the man. Men could divorce their wives, but there was no provision for a woman to divorce her husband.

• Divorce involved a man giving a woman a written *"certificate of divorce,"* placing it in her hand, and sending her out of his house. This certificate of divorce could be given for many different reasons, depending on how a man or his particular circle of family and friends defined the terms *"finds no favor in his eyes"* and *"uncleanness in her."* There were some Jews who believed that uncleanness referred only to sexual infidelity. There were others who claimed that any kind of "disfavor" that a woman evoked in her husband's eyes could be considered grounds for divorce. In some instances, women were divorced for keeping an unclean house, for habitually cooking food in a way the husband didn't like, or for being argumentative. Some even allowed divorce to be given if a man found his wife to be "less favorable" than someone else he happened to meet. There were no set definitions for *"no favor"* or *"uncleanness"* when it came to divorce.

• A divorced woman could be married to another man, but if she found herself divorced or a widow in the future, she could not return to her first husband. God's Word stood against a musical-chairs approach to marriage.

The only other commandment related to divorce and remarriage in the Old Testament is a commandment for those select few who were the high priests. The high priest was commanded to take an Israelite virgin as his wife; he was not allowed to marry a harlot, a divorced woman, a widow, or a "defiled woman." (See Leviticus 21:14.)

What Jesus Taught

The New Testament teaching of Jesus is much harder. We read, as part of the Sermon on the Mount, this statement:

> *Furthermore it has been said, "Whoever divorces his wife, let him give her a certificate of divorce." But I say to you that whoever divorces his wife for any reason except sexual*

immorality causes her to commit adultery; and whoever marries a woman who is divorced commits adultery.

(Matthew 5:31–32)

Jesus defined the *"no favor"* and "unclean" issues that were left undefined by the Law of Moses. He said that divorce was to be allowed only in cases of sexual immorality, which also has been translated as sexual infidelity or adultery.

One day a Pharisee came to Jesus and asked Him, *"Is it lawful for a man to divorce his wife?"* (Mark 10:2). The Pharisees were those who placed the highest priority on keeping the Law—not only the Law of Moses, but all the laws developed by the rabbis through the ages. This Pharisee asked this question as a *test* of Jesus; he wanted to see if what He said lined up with what the Pharisees believed.

Jesus replied, *"What did Moses command you?"* (v. 3). Jesus was moving the argument away from what all the rabbis said to what Moses said.

The Pharisee responded, *"Moses permitted a man to write a certificate of divorce, and to dismiss her"* (v. 4).

Jesus answered,

> *Because of the hardness of your heart he wrote you this precept. But from the beginning of the creation, God "made them male and female." "For this reason a man shall leave his father and mother and be joined to his wife, and the two shall become one flesh"; so then they are no longer two, but one flesh. Therefore what God has joined together, let not man separate.* (vv. 5–9)

Later Jesus' disciples asked Him about this same matter, and He said to them, *"Whoever divorces his wife and marries another commits adultery against her. And if a woman divorces her husband and marries another, she commits adultery"* (vv. 11–12).

Let me point out to you several things about these verses:

• Divorce is a matter of the heart. It is because we allow our hearts to become hardened that we seek a divorce. God's higher desire is that two people who marry stay together for the rest of their lives.

• If you divorce your spouse and remarry, you are joining yourself to someone who is not the one whom God joined to you. You are committing "adultery" against that one whom God joined to you. Nothing is said about the spouse who is divorced against his or her will; the "instigator" of the divorce, the one who sought the divorce, is the one who Jesus said was violating God's highest purpose for marriage.

> God's desire is that two people who marry stay together for the rest of their lives.

• We are to seek to remain one flesh in our marriages and not separate. *"What God has joined together, let not man separate"* (Mark 10:9). When God joins together two people in marriage, they are regarded as one physical entity in His eyes—one social unit, one family, one "body."

Marriage was taken very seriously by Jesus. He saw it as something created by God *"from the beginning of creation"* (2 Peter 3:4). He saw marriage as being an integral part of God's plan and purpose.

People state many reasons for why they are seeking a divorce. What Jesus calls us to do is to seek out reasons that we should stay together!

Accept God's Plan

In the account of this passage recorded in Matthew, Jesus' disciples said to Him, *"If such is the case of the man with his wife, it is better not to marry"* (Matthew 19:10). In other words, they were saying, "If that's the case—if I have to stay in a marriage no matter what—I'd be better off never marrying."

Jesus replied,

> *All cannot accept this saying, but only those to whom it has been given: for there are eunuchs who were born thus from their mother's womb, and there are eunuchs who were made eunuchs by men, and there are eunuchs who have*

made themselves eunuchs for the kingdom of heaven's sake.
He who is able to accept it, let him accept it.

(Matthew 19:11–12)

Jesus was noting that there are some men who have no sexual
drive or ability—from birth, as the result of
castration, or who have taken a vow before
the Lord. But, Jesus said, for those who desire
normal sexual activity, *"Let him accept it."* In
other words, if you want to have a sexual
relationship with the opposite sex, play by
God's rules for marriage. If you want to get
married, accept God's plan for marriage.

If you want to have a sexual relationship with the opposite sex, play by God's rules.

If you are looking for an excuse to justify leaving your spouse,
you will find it.

But if you are looking for reasons to stay with your spouse, you
also will find them.

What are you looking for?

God Calls Us to Peace

There is only one other passage of admonition in the New
Testament directly related to divorce.

> *Now to the married I command, yet not I but the Lord: A*
> *wife is not to depart from her husband. But even if she does*
> *depart, let her remain unmarried or be reconciled to her*
> *husband. And a husband is not to divorce his wife. But to*
> *the rest I, not the Lord, say: If any brother has a wife who*
> *does not believe, and she is willing to live with him, let*
> *him not divorce her. And a woman who has a husband who*
> *does not believe, if he is willing to live with her, let her not*
> *divorce him. For the unbelieving husband is sanctified by*
> *the wife, and the unbelieving wife is sanctified by the hus-*
> *band; otherwise your children would be unclean, but now*
> *they are holy. But if the unbeliever departs, let him depart;*
> *a brother or a sister is not under bondage in such cases. But*
> *God has called us to peace.* (1 Corinthians 7:10–15)

The apostle Paul was writing primarily to new Christian believers, many of whom were married to those who had not yet

accepted Christ. He told them not to leave their spouses because they were unbelievers. But, at the same time, he said that if the unbeliever in the relationship chose to depart, to let him or her do so in peace. In those cases, the believer should not consider him- or herself to be under any bondage. In other words, he or she is free to remarry.

The better course, said the apostle Paul, is to stay married if at all possible because then you, as a believer, will have maximum opportunity to be a witness to your spouse. There's no greater place to show the love and mercy of God to an unbeliever than in your home. Your spouse, children, and other family members should be the ones who experience the greatest "witness" you have for Christ.

The Bible gives us permission to divorce a spouse who has committed adultery. The Bible does not *require* a marriage to end in the aftermath of adultery or infidelity. Rather, a person *may* divorce a spouse who is unfaithful.

The apostle Paul called church members to live in peace, and if a couple can work through an issue of infidelity in their marriage and come to a peaceful understanding and a new beginning, then I believe they are wise to do so. God's ultimate best is for marriages to be healed, restored, and strengthened.

Facing a Violation of Your Marriage Vows

Adultery can be a devastating blow to marriage. It does very serious damage to trust. I believe that's the reason Jesus taught that, in cases of adultery, it's permissible for a couple to divorce. Sometimes the breach of trust and the feelings of betrayal run so deep that they cannot be healed in a relationship. On the other hand, adultery does not mean an automatic death sentence for a marriage. Some people are able to work through the fact that an affair has taken place; they are able to forgive and make changes and move forward in their marriage.

> God's ultimate best is for marriages to be healed, restored, and strengthened.

If you make the decision to stay with your spouse after your spouse has committed adultery, you face not only the challenge of forgiving your spouse, but also the challenge of moving forward in your relationship with a spirit of ongoing forgiveness.

Don't bring up the past, no matter how tempted you may be to do so. Leave the past in the past. Don't hold back from your sexual relationship with your spouse. You may not realize it, but in withholding sex from your spouse, you are trying to punish your spouse—and that is not an act of forgiveness. Your spouse will feel further hurt and rejection, and he or she may feel even more justified about the adulterous behavior.

There is a season for you to feel hurt and to get over your hurt. But you need to move through that season and then move on, acting in relationship to your spouse as if the adultery never happened. If you can't do that, then leave. If you choose to stay in the marriage, this "forgetting" is a must. Your marriage is headed for destruction if you continue to keep the issue of adultery at the center of your relationship.

One of the greatest challenges you will face is getting the "other person" out of your own mind. If you continue to imagine what the other person was like or what your spouse and the other person were like together, you will live in torment. How do you get this other person out of your mind? Get into God's Word. Get a strong image of what God desires *you* to be and what God says you are as His beloved child. Get a strong image for what your marriage can be like—and then live in that image.

Abusive Behavior

A very close second to adultery is abuse. Abusive behavior can destroy a marriage as quickly as adultery can.

If your spouse is abusing you, get away from that person. That person is dangerous, both physically and emotionally. There's something destructive in that person; there's anger, hatred, and bitterness that haven't been healed.

Many people think wives are the only people who are abused in marriage. That isn't at all the case. More husbands than you know are beat up by their wives, physically as well as emotionally. They are scratched, kicked, pounded with fists, and given black eyes. They have things thrown at them, as well as angry, abusive, vulgar words thrown at them. Walk away from that. Don't put up with that.

I'm not saying to divorce. I'm saying to put some distance between you and that person. Let tempers cool. Get some counseling so you can heal emotionally and spiritually. Get into God's Word and see what God's Word has to say about anger, hatred, and violence. Develop some skills for dealing with the situation. Spend some time in prayer and intercession—not only for your spouse, but also for yourself so that you might be healed. God never intended for you to be walked on by another person. He never intended for another person to take his or her frustrations, lack of self-worth, anger, and bitterness out on you.

Above all, stop blaming yourself for the abuse you are receiving. That's a lie from the devil. You may want to change some things in the way you respond to an abusive person, but in ninety-nine out of a hundred cases, *you* are not the cause of the abuse. There's something else going on in the abuser's heart. There's a selfishness, a seething frustration, a fighting spirit to gain feelings of self-worth; there's an anger, a bitterness. It's wrong for you to live in guilt for the sin in somebody else's life. Ask God to free you from that guilt. Ask God to remove all feelings of shame and guilt from you and to replace those feelings with feelings of strength, confidence, and purity.

Addictive Behavior

If you are living with a person who is addicted to any kind of chemical substance, that addiction is going to influence your relationship. Before you can have a normal, godly sexual relationship, your addicted spouse is going to have to be set free from that addiction. Intervene on his or her behalf—get some help; take some action; do what you can to help this person get the medical, psychological, and spiritual help that's necessary for genuine and lasting healing.

Be aware that cocaine or crack does what an illicit lover does. A lover takes a spouse's emotions, his or her soul. So does cocaine. It influences a person's desires and takes authority over his or her will. A spouse who is addicted to crack always gives that crack his or her time, money, energy, and "love."

Cocaine, heroin, or any other drug causes a person to do ungodly things in order to pursue the use of the drug. Some steal or sell their bodies to get money to buy the drug; some lie and cheat in order to hide their addiction; some abandon their spouse and their children in favor of the drug.

A spouse who is using drugs needs to be confronted: "Do you want our marriage to work? If you do, then you need to give up this lover. You need to walk away from that crack house. You need to quit holding on to that crack pipe and sucking on it. You need to quit spending your money on the drug dealer, taking food out of your children's mouths."

Confront the drug user just as you would confront a spouse who was cheating on you.

I have a corollary to the concluding line of the marriage vows: "Let no man or woman or any freaky thing put a marriage asunder." That includes drugs!

Do You Want to Stay Married?

The most important question you can ask in these areas, as well as in all other areas involving conflict, is this: do you want to stay married? Do you want to stay in the relationship?

A woman once told me that she had received wonderful marriage advice when she was in college. One of her professors had said, "My wife and I have counseled people for twenty-five years. We have come to one conclusion about why people stay together. People stay married because they want to be married more than they want to be unmarried."

People stay married because they want to be married more than they want to be unmarried.

That man was absolutely right!

216

Marriage is an act of your will. It's a choice you make. But it's not a choice that just one person in a marriage can make. Both of you must want to be married to each other more than you want to be unmarried and live without each other. If you are married and both of you want to stay married, then you'll find a way to work through even these very difficult problems and stay married. If you don't want to be married any longer—either one of you or both of you—then there's nothing anybody can do to patch up your marriage and cause you to stay together. It all comes down to agreement. You have to *agree* to be married to each other.

Conclusion

Walking in Harmony toward God's Rewards

God's ideal for your marriage is that you walk in harmony toward great rewards that He holds out to you. This is true for every area of your life, including your marriage.

If you sow to the righteousness of your spouse and build up your own godly behavior, you will reap a reward in your marriage. God's Word is clear on this:

> Do not be deceived, God is not mocked; for whatever a man sows, that he will also reap. For he who sows to his flesh will of the flesh reap corruption, but he who sows to the Spirit will of the Spirit reap everlasting life. And let us not grow weary while doing good, for in due season we shall reap if we do not lose heart. Therefore, as we have opportunity, let us do good to all, especially to those who are of the household of faith.   (Galatians 6:7–10)

Don't be deceived. If you sow love, patience, and kindness into your spouse, you will reap love, patience, and kindness from your spouse. If you do good to your spouse—if you speak good words that build up and edify your spouse, do good deeds for your spouse, and live out a good reputation before the world regarding your spouse—you *will* reap a harvest of good in your marriage. The harvest may not be today. It may take a while for your seeds of love, patience, kindness, and goodness to grow into a full-blown crop of love, patience, kindness, and goodness, but that day of harvest will come if you don't lose heart and give up.

What are the rewards God has for a marriage that operates according to His plan? That marriage will last. It will endure. That couple will stay together.

God will reward the husband and wife in that marriage with deep feelings of fulfillment, satisfaction, and joy.

God will reward that husband and wife with an even deeper love and compassion for each other.

These rewards come to us as we *consistently* pursue God's plan for marriage. It is what you consistently do that will be reflected in your life and in your marriage. If you consistently pray, your life will be marked by your consistent prayer. If you are consistently angry, your life is going to be marked by consistent frustration, poor relationships, and bitterness.

> It is what you consistently do that will be reflected in your life and in your marriage.

If you tell me about your marriage, "My marriage is continually full of trouble," then I have to ask, "What are you continually doing to create an environment in which trouble is constantly present?"

If you tell me, "We just don't seem to be able to understand each other," then I have to ask, "What is the habitual nature of your communication? What is your habit for spending time with each other?"

We must consistently revisit our marriage vows and our level of commitment.

We must consistently face the present reality of a problem in our marriage.

We must be consistent in our faithfulness.

We must consistently communicate.

We must consistently be trustworthy and truthful.

We must consistently learn how to be a better spouse.

We must consistently work on our friendship with our spouse.

We must consistently forgive.

We must consistently work at controlling our anger.

We must consistently pray for our spouse and our marriage.

Give no toehold to the devil to enter your relationship by failing to keep the commandments of marriage consistently.

Nobody ever gets to the point in marriage where he or she can stop watching and praying. There's no point in marriage where you no longer need to submit to God's will.

The devil can always slip a thought into your mind. You can always feel impulses and desires. You don't become blind to the opposite sex when you get married. Your thoughts and desires and your impulses all need to be submitted to God day after day after day.

Renew your commitment to do things God's way, no matter what. No matter what circumstances, no matter what situations, no matter how your spouse treats you or responds to you—*no matter what.*

When you render the proper attitude toward your spouse, and when you behave toward your spouse in a consistently godly manner, you *will* be rewarded by God. The Bible says,

> *Whatever you do, do it heartily, as to the Lord and not to men, knowing that from the Lord you will receive the reward of the inheritance; for you serve the Lord Christ. But he who does wrong will be repaid for what he has done, and there is no partiality.* (Colossians 3:23–25)

All conflicts can be resolved...with God's help.

All blessings and rewards can be received...with our obedience to God's plan.

A marriage can be a wonderful thing...with God involved in every facet of it!

OTHER POWERFUL **B**OOKS

Distributed through
Whitaker House

The Disease Called Comparisonitis
Darrell L. Hines

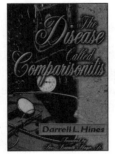

If you're trying to be someone else or receive approval from others, you could lose your mind and miss your purpose! It's time to discover your true identity and the purpose that God has for your life.

ISBN: 0-96775-350-3 • Trade • 29 pages

A Lifestyle of Healing
Pamela M. Hines

When you receive Jesus Christ as your Lord and Savior, you also receive all the benefits that accompany your decision. Healing is one of those benefits. This book provides a practical yet spiritual approach to obtaining and maintaining divine health.

ISBN: 0-96775-352-X • Trade • 40 pages

Let Them Have Dominion
Darrell and Pamela Hines

In the marriage relationship, God has given a place of authority to both husbands and wives. Drawing on more than twenty years of marital and ministry experience, the authors reveal God's purpose for a husband and wife who sense God's call unitedly upon their lives.

ISBN: 0-96775-351-1 • Trade • 86 pages

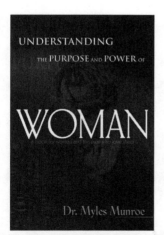

OTHER POWERFUL OOKS
from Whitaker House

Crazy House, Sane House
George & Jeannie Bloomer

There are two kinds of marriage you can end up with: good or bad, crazy or sane. The end result is up to you! If marriage is in your near future, or even if you've been married for decades, don't wait another minute! Discover the keys to building a strong house, a strong marriage, and a strong future!

ISBN: 0-88368-726-7 • Trade • 144 pages

Even with My Issues
Dr. Wanda A. Turner

The enemy will try anything to prevent you from moving beyond your issues. But you can be free of the shame and bondage of your issues. Dr. Wanda Turner invites you on the most challenging journey you will ever take—a journey from rejection to acceptance, from fear to faith, from a shattered life to wholeness. Discover how you, too, can be entirely set free.

ISBN: 0-88368-673-2 • Trade • 160 pages